RED GUIDE

Western Scotland

Oban   Fort William
Skye   The Hebrides

Edited by
Reginald J. W. Hammond

Seventeenth Edition—Reprint

WARD LOCK LIMITED

116 BAKER STREET, LONDON W.1

Printed in Great Britain by
Billing & Sons Limited, Guildford and London

Contents

CONTENTS

Illustrations

THE RED GUIDES

With Maps, Plans and Illustrations

Aberystwyth
Anglesey and North Wales

Barmouth, etc.
Bournemouth and District
Broads
Bude and North Cornwall

Channel Islands
Cornwall: North
Cornwall: South
Cornwall: West
Cotswolds
Cromer, Sheringham

Devon: North-west
Devon: South
Devon: South-east
Dorset Coast

Eastbourne, Seaford, etc.
Exeter and S.E. Devon
Exmoor and Doone Country

Falmouth and S. Cornwall

Ilfracombe and N.W. Devon
Isle of Man
Isle of Wight

Kent Coast

Lake District
Llandudno, Colwyn Bay
London
Lyme Regis and District
Lynton and Lynmouth

New Forest
Newquay and N. Cornwall
Norfolk, North

Peak District
Penzance and W. Cornwall

St. Ives and W. Cornwall
Stratford upon Avon
Sussex Coast: East
Sussex Coast: West
Swanage, Corfe, etc.

Tenby and South Wales
Thames, inc. Oxford
Torquay and District

Wales, N. (Northn. Section)
Wales, N. (Southn. Section)
Wales, South
Weymouth and District
Wye Valley

Yorkshire Coast
Yorkshire Dales

SCOTLAND

Aberdeen, Deeside, etc.
Edinburgh and District
Glasgow and the Clyde
Highlands

Inverness, Strathpeffer, etc.
Northern Scotland
Oban, Fort William, etc.
Western Scotland

RED TOURIST GUIDES

Baddeley's Guide to the Lake District
The Complete Guide to Scotland

The Complete Guide to Ireland
The Complete Guide to Wales

WARD, LOCK & CO., LIMITED

Introduction

Western Scotland—Books to Read—Sport—Angling—National Forest Parks—Walking and Climbing—Clothing—To Scotland by Rail and Sea—Road and Air Services—Hotels

That part of Scotland described in this Guide is unsurpassed in the British Isles for the grandeur of its scenery, in which mountains, fresh- and salt-water lochs, islands, and sea are predominant. From Cruachan and Ben Nevis to the "far Coolins," from Loch Lomond and Loch Awe to Loch Ness and Loch Maree, from Loch Fyne to Loch Torridon and Gruinard Bay, from Islay and Mull and Skye to the Outer Hebrides, it comprises a region of irresistible appeal to the rover, be he young or no longer young, to the student or the sportsman, artist or archæologist, climber or hiker, motorist or sea-voyager—in short, to the tourist and holiday-maker of every type and nationality. The area covered in the following pages can boast not only the highest mountain (Ben Nevis) and the three largest lakes (Lomond, Ness, Awe) in Britain, but the deepest lake (Morar), the longest sea-lochs (Fyne, Linnhe), the biggest islands (Long Island and Skye), world-famous places of pilgrimage, like the sacred isle of Iona, historic scenes such as Glencoe and Glenfinnan, vast wild National Forest Parks and our first Nature Reserve (Beinn Eighe).

On the mainland the two principal centres for exploring Western Scotland are Oban and Fort William. Oban, indeed, is so fortunately placed that few towns in Britain can offer such variety of excursions by road, rail, and sea. The excursion to Staffa and Iona is the finest day trip that can be taken off the coast of Great Britain, and the excursion from Oban to Ballachulish and up Glencoe by road lies through some of the most impressive scenery in Scotland.

The West of Scotland season is at its height in August. Visitors who can choose their time should go earlier in the year. In May, June, and July not only are the days longer—in June one can

often read by "daylight" almost until midnight—but the glens have a greater freshness than in later months. The motor, train and steamer summer services generally extend from June to September; in the earlier and later months there is no over-crowding either when travelling or at the hotels. June is perhaps the best month of the twelve. In October the glorious autumn tints are at their finest.

Highland Gatherings

A unique feature of the Scottish season is the series of "Gatherings" or "Games," some of which have a world-wide celebrity. At these gatherings one sees the Scot in all the pride of kilt and tartan; the pipes are heard from morn till eve and the national dances take a prominent part in the programme. The sporting events include tossing the caber—the stem of a fir tree—putting the weight and other feats requiring not only strength but skill for their proper performance.

The "Games" season extends from June to September, in which month is held the Argyllshire Gathering at Oban. Mull Highland Games take place at Tobermory in July, those of Skye at Portree in August, like the Cowal Highland Gathering at Dunoon. Sheep-dog Trials are also a feature of the season.

Books to Read

So many books deal with, or have their scenes laid in, the Western Highlands that we cannot do more than mention a few of those most worth reading or re-reading.

The works of Sir Walter Scott, of course, demand first place: his *Lady of the Lake* first attracted visitors to the Trossachs; the *Lord of the Isles* was the last of his verse romances; and the *Legend of Montrose* and *Rob Roy* are among the Waverley novels which may be read with appreciation while visiting Western Scotland.

8

In modern times the mantle of Scott may be said to have descended on Neil Munro, whose *John Splendid*, *Doom Castle*, and other novels deal thrillingly and accurately with Argyll, especially the region around Inveraray. Another interpreter of Scottish history is D. K. Broster, whose trilogy *The Flight of the Heron*, *The Gleam in the North*, and *The Dark Mile* recalls the stirring events of the '45. Marjorie Bowen's *Glen of Weeping* is, of course, Glencoe. R. L. Stevenson's *Kidnapped* and *Catriona* gain fresh interest on visits to Appin and Rannoch Moor. In lighter vein is John Buchan's *John Macnab*, and in *Whisky Galore* and other stories Sir Compton Mackenzie entertainingly depicts Hebridean scenes and characters in war-time and post-war days.

Among innumerable "travel books" dealing with the Western Highlands and Islands may be mentioned works by Seton Gordon, A. A. MacGregor and Iain F. Anderson. Visitors to Skye should read J. A. MacCulloch's *Misty Isle of Skye*, Alexander Smith's *A Summer in Skye*, and B. H. Humble's *Tramping in Skye*. For Oban district in particular Hugh Shedden's *The Story of Lorn, the Isles, and Oban* is valuable.

For mountain-lovers the very best companions are the Scottish Mountaineering Club's *Guides* to *Ben Nevis*, the *Western Highlands*, the *Central Highlands*, to *Glencoe and Ardgour*, and to *Skye*. Ward Lock's *Complete Scotland* is a thoroughly comprehensive and modern guide to the whole country, from the Borders to the Shetland Islands and from Aberdeen to St. Kilda.

Sport

There are few villages without a golf course and a green for the game of bowls. In this particular area full-length links are not so numerous or so well known as on the Clyde or on the East Coast, but Oban has a sporting 18-hole course at Glencruitten, and Machrihanish attracts many golfers. At Oban, Fort William, and elsewhere are public tennis courts. Shinty (or *Camanachd*), a Highland game like hockey, is popular and is well worth watching.

Many hotels provide shooting for their guests, but some of the best shootings are now let to small syndicates, membership including residence at a shooting lodge. Here and there such lodges have been turned into hotels.

9

Angling

For trout fishing in Scotland, the season is from March 15 to October 6 (both dates inclusive). Salmon fishing (rod) generally is open from February 11 to October 31, but begins and closes earlier or later on several rivers and lochs.

North-Western Scotland holds out attractions of its own to the angler, so enrapturing are the surroundings, regardless of the catch. Salmon, as well as brown trout, may be caught in innumerable streams and lochs, but sea-trout offer the best sport of all, this region (mainland and isles alike) being among their favourite haunts.

The hotels often cater specially for anglers and in the neighbourhood of open waters, such as Loch Awe, there is no lack of choice or comfort or company—but the fisher who prefers to get away as much as possible from his fellow-men will usually find accommodation to his liking in remoter parts. Where there are lochs—and where aren't there lochs in the West Highlands? —the hotels have boats and knowledgeable gillies available, at charges which, if not cheap, are never prohibitive to the enthusiast of the rod. Some hotels have private lochans or stretches of river which guests may fish free or at charges varying according to circumstances.

The Scottish Tourist Board (Rutland Place, Edinburgh) issues annually (3s. 6d.) a helpful guide to open waters, entitled *Scotland for Fishing*. The angling clubs or tackle sellers may be consulted for local conditions. In the following pages angling notes will be found among the details given regarding places described.

National Forest Parks

The region covered in this *Guide* is fortunate in the possession of a number of National Forest Parks, which not only present wide and wild stretches of moorland and mountain range to the tramper, the camper, and the climber, but offer happy hunting grounds to the botanist, the zoologist and the geologist, the artist and the photographer, the antiquarian and the nature-lover of every kind.

(1) South of Oban, between Loch Long and Loch Fyne, lies the **Argyll National Forest Park** (58,000 acres). The Ardgoil portion of it belongs to the City of Glasgow, the remainder to the Forestry Commission. At *Benmore House* (7 miles north of Dunoon) are situated the **Younger Botanic Gardens,** jointly administered by the Forestry Commission and the Ministry of Public Building and Works (*charge*). These contain a unique collection of flowering shrubs (notably rhododendrons of some 200 different species).

(2) To the north, skirting Loch Alsh and Loch Duich, the **Balmacara, Glomach,** and **Kintail** estates (together covering about 25,000 acres) of the National Trust for Scotland now maintain in its natural state another of the grandest areas in Scotland.

(3) To the north-west the National Trust's estates of **Glencoe and Dalness** (12,000 acres) preserve in similar fashion a district of scenic splendour, steeped in history and legend, with unfailing attractions for the motor-borne tourist, the energetic rock-climber and the skier alike.

(4) To the east of Oban, in the romantic Trossachs and Rob Roy country, is the **Queen Elizabeth Forest Park** (over 41,000 acres) which includes an extensive part of the area between Ben Lomond, Aberfoyle, and Loch Achray, so perennially appealing to the tourist.

In or near all these Parks there are Youth Hostels, and some have camping grounds. National Nature Reserves in the area include Rannoch Moor, Beinn Eighe (Torridon), Rhum, and St. Kilda.

Walking and Climbing

Boots should be nailed—rubber soles are apt to be treacherous on wet rock or on grass. Carry a good map and a reliable compass and in reading the map do not attend only to details of route but study the conformation of the ground over which you pass—such information may be invaluable in helping you to find your way down in case of mist. Also in case of mist or other causes of delay, it is always wise to take an emergency ration—such as a good slab of chocolate—and to *reserve* it until one is definitely on a beaten track.

Midges, clegs, and other winged pests are apt to prove a trial in summer, and it is well to carry a midge repellent.

With its long hours of daylight and its more dependable weather conditions, June is the best month for walking in Scotland. Later in the year routes are apt to be restricted by

11

grouse-shooting, deer-stalking, and the like. Against arbitrary restrictions the Rights-of-Way Society has fought with much success, and its signpost is an increasingly familiar and welcome feature, but strangers should note that the right on such routes is confined to the actual paths and does not assume leave to wander at will.

Walkers will find the hostels of the *Scottish Youth Hostels Association* of great service. There is a chain of hostels from Glasgow to Oban, Glencoe, Fort William, Kyle of Lochalsh, and Gairloch, and no fewer than four in Skye. Full particulars may be obtained from S.Y.H.A., 7 Bruntsfield Crescent, Edinburgh, 10. Mountaineering and Ski Clubs have several huts for their members.

The routes described in our pages are nearly all well within the powers of the average walker, and in clear weather are free from danger, but the novice would be well advised to keep to the beaten tracks and to gain experience before attempting routes or climbs which may be beyond his powers of endurance: this warning is emphatically necessary with regard to the Coolins (where the compass cannot always be relied upon). The greatest danger is from mist. If overtaken suddenly, it is best to remain still for a while, for the mist may pass as quickly as it came. Those proposing a tour extending to parts of Scotland not dealt with in this Guide should see Ward Lock's *Complete Scotland*, in which every important walking route is indicated.

Clothing

When considering the question of suitable clothing, the intending visitor should bear in mind the motor and steamer trips which will probably be undertaken. On such occasions additional garments will be found very acceptable, and one's pleasure may be spoilt without them. For excursions like those to Staffa or Loch Scavaig stout footwear with low heels is advised. Generally speaking, ordinary clothing should be warmer than for the south of England. Waterproofs should be really waterproof— the light "mac" is of little use in a heavy storm.

Railway Facilities

Those coming from England have the choice of three overland

routes to the northern side of the Border. They are the West Coast Route (*London Midland Region* from London); the East Coast Route (*Eastern Region* from London); and the Midland Route (*London Midland Region* to Carlisle; thereafter to Glasgow, Central Station, *via* Kilmarnock, or to Edinburgh *via* Hawick). The West Coast Route is the oldest route to Scotland, and the most direct to Oban. The distance from London to Edinburgh is 393 miles by the East Coast; to Glasgow 402 miles, and to Oban 504 by the West Coast. For descriptions of the routes onward to Oban, *see* pp. 19-26.

Through carriages are run on the principal expresses; restaurant-cars are attached to most of these, and the night trains have sleeping-cars. At all times it is advisable—and in the season essential—to book in advance. Nightly (except Saturday) first and second class through carriages and sleeping-cars run from London (Kings Cross) to Fort William; likewise from Fort William (except Sunday) to London (King's Cross).

In Scotland the East Coast route to Oban is *via* Edinburgh and Glasgow, but by the Midland and West Coast routes one can go from Carlisle *via* Carstairs, or Kilmarnock to Glasgow and from there to Oban.

The West Highland Line leaves Glasgow by the north bank of the Clyde, thence runs northward beside the Gare Loch, Loch Long and Loch Lomond to Crianlarich whence it crosses the bleak Rannoch Moor, and subsequently descends to Glen Spean, in which it turns west for Fort William, continuing westward to Mallaig (for steamer services).

The Oban line diverges from the West Highland line at Crianlarich and runs westward *via* Dalmally, alongside Loch Awe, thence Connel Ferry, before winding down through Glencruitten to Oban.

To the far North and North-west the rail route is *via* Perth Inverness and Dingwall, whence a branch line runs westward to, Kyle of Lochalsh for the ferry to Skye and steamers to the Outer Hebrides.

It should be noted that few of the local services and only a limited number of the main line services operate on Sundays.

To Scotland by Sea

Latest information may be obtained at the usual travel agencies.
Dublin to Glasgow, by *Burns and Laird Lines*, 56 Robertson Street, Glasgow, C.2.

Belfast to Glasgow (daylight service *via* Ardrossan in summer), by *Burns and Laird Lines*; or by the Caledonian Steam Packet Company's short sea route, *via* Larne and Stranraer.

Glasgow to Oban (*see* pp. 21-6).

Road Services

Although large areas in the district described are remote from railways, there are bus services (sometimes understandably infrequent) to almost every place accessible by road. Generally speaking, these services run in connection with the trains and boats, but time-tables should, of course, be consulted.

Time Tables. British Railways issue time tables for the Scottish Region (with connecting services by motor and steamer). Besides their Steamer Time Tables, MacBraynes publish separate Motor Coach Time Tables for their services in different areas—Northern, Southern, and Islands.

Air Services

In vivid contrast to the simple, almost primitive, life of some of the outer islands are the air services which keep them in close touch with the mainland. Barra has been brought within two hours of Glasgow; Lewis within an hour of Inverness. Every morning (except Sunday) a B.E.A. plane goes from Glasgow (Abbotsinch Airport) to Benbecula and Stornoway, returning in the afternoon; another goes likewise to Campbeltown and Islay. On several week-days there is an air service between Glasgow, Tiree and Barra. Inverness is in daily (except Sunday) connection with Glasgow and with Stornoway. Abbotsinch Airport is also in daily communication with Belfast and (by Aer Lingus) with Dublin. Prestwick is, of course, notable as a transatlantic and international airport, with services to and from America and Europe. Details of services can be ascertained at any tourist office or from British European Airways.

Hotels

The hotel accommodation is admirable on the whole, but is taxed to the utmost during the season. To avoid disappointment it is advisable always to book in advance. As a rule, the charges are reasonable, especially when remoteness and shortness of the season are taken into account. In the following pages, the names of hotels are given, *in italics*, within brackets, in descending order of magnitude or tariff. A National Register of Accommodation, *Where to Stay in Scotland* (3*s*. 6*d*.), is published annually by the Scottish Tourist Board (Rutland Place, Edinburgh).

Motoring

Motoring in Western Scotland is unlike motoring in almost any other part of Britain on account of the manner in which the roads are made to wind both by mountains and by lochs—especially the sea lochs, which often penetrate far inland and cause very considerable detours. However, as much of the best scenery can be viewed from the roads, this habit of winding obviously has its compensations, and in certain cases stout ferry boats capable of carrying cars and caravans provide short-cuts across the lochs.

The long and beautiful road (A82) from Tyndrum to Inverness *via* Glencoe and Fort William (as reconstructed in 1928-34) forms one of the finest highways in Britain. For those hurrying north by this route the one drawback is the necessity of rounding Loch Leven, at the foot of Glencoe, or of crossing it by Ballachulish Ferry.

Few of the roads in the district are of the high standard of this great highway, but progress has been made with the rebuilding of the narrow and tortuous but enchanting road (A830), westward from Fort William to Arisaig and Mallaig. In outlying parts, such as Lewis, West Highland roads (other than trunk ones) are liable to fall into a deplorable state, owing to very costly maintenance, weather conditions, bus and lorry traffic, and other factors.

Motorists proposing to explore some of the more remote corners are advised to see to oil, petrol, etc., before leaving the modern highways with their frequent filling stations.

Ferries

Motorists in Western Scotland should note that a number of ferries available for pedestrians or cyclists are unable to carry cars. It is also to be remembered that ferries near the coast may be influenced by the tide in the regularity of their services and that, especially in the summer months, considerable delay may be entailed by congestion of traffic or other causes.

For details of the Skye ferries, *see* p. 129.

Other ferries which may be noted by motorists are that at **Ballachulish** (near the foot of Glencoe)—a brief crossing which obviates driving round the head of Loch Leven (*see* p. 102); and the neighbouring ferry across Loch Linnhe from **Corran to Ardgour** (*see* p. 94), which saves those bound for the extreme West a much longer detour *via* Fort William and Loch Eil.

Loch Etive, running far inland just north of Oban, may be crossed by the cantilever bridge at **Connel** (p. 42), and Dornie ferry on Loch Duich has been superseded by a bridge on the Kyle of Lochalsh road from the south (p. 120).

It is possible to take cars over to some of **The Western Isles** by steamer from Oban, Kyle of Lochalsh or Mallaig. Arrangements must be made in advance, and motorists must bear in mind that the state of the tide and the difference between deck level and pier level may not permit of motors being run aboard or ashore.

Motor Routes from England

Of the seven points at which the Border may be crossed by main road the most convenient, so far as travellers to Oban are concerned, is probably that (A74) forking to the left a mile or two north of Carlisle and entering Scotland at **Gretna Green,** long famous for its runaway "Blacksmith" marriages. Hence a fine road runs up by Lockerbie and Beattock and then down Clydesdale to Abington, where there is a choice of route. Those who propose to go through **Glasgow** bear off to the left (by A74); the right-hand road (A73) runs *via* Lanark, Carluke, Airdrie, and Denny and the industrial belt between Forth and Clyde and brings one to Cumbernauld, on the Glasgow road to **Stirling** (A80), whence the route *via* Callander is described on pp. 20-1.

Those who desire to use the Loch Lomond or Loch Long routes, and yet wish to avoid the busy streets of Glasgow, should leave the Abington-Glasgow road (A74) beyond Lesmahagow and make for Erskine Ferry (by A726) *via* Strathaven and Paisley. Alternatively, one can bear left at Gretna Green (by A75) for **Dumfries.** Hence the road is northward *via* Thornhill,

Sanquhar, Cumnock, Kilmarnock, and Paisley to **Erskine Ferry**, across the Clyde to Old Kilpatrick. This ferry operates daily from early morning till 10 or 11 p.m. Embarkation is easy: the crossing takes only two or three minutes: the charges are moderate. On leaving the ferry turn westward and so *via* Balloch as described on p. 21.

Motorists crossing the Border towards its eastern end have the choice of four roads. That *via* Berwick-on-Tweed follows the coast more or less closely to Edinburgh; those *via* (*a*) Coldstream, (*b*) Carter Bar-Jedburgh, and (*c*) Carter Bar-Hawick run more directly to Edinburgh.

For Stirling—and so to Oban—leave Edinburgh by the west end of Princes Street and the Corstorphine Road (A8); or if a glimpse of the Forth Bridge is desired by Dean Bridge and the Queensferry Road. The two routes unite at Linlithgow, whence the way is clear by Falkirk to Stirling.

Those bound for Fort William, for Skye, or places on the mainland west of the Great Glen will make for the southern end of the fine Glencoe road near Tyndrum. At the lower end of Glencoe either cross Loch Leven by Ballachulish Ferry or drive round the head of the Loch by Kinlochleven. From Fort William the road to Inverness through the Great Glen serves roads running out to the West coast; there is also an adventurous road (now, as a Trunk Road, being improved) to Arisaig and Mallaig.

For Skye one can reach the ferry at Kyle of Lochalsh by one of the roads running west from the Great Glen at Invergarry or Invermoriston; or run north to Inverness either by the Great Glen or by the Great North Road *via* Pitlochry, Newtonmore, Aviemore and Carrbridge, and from Inverness proceed westward by Muir of Ord and Garve to Strome Ferry (p. 125; no crossing on Sunday) and Kyle of Lochalsh.

Car-Sleeper Services. These services, carrying cars and passengers by rail, and thus saving the long drive to Scotland are available between:

London (King's Cross)—Edinburgh (Waverley).
London (Kensington Olympia)—Perth.
Newhaven—Stirling.
Sutton Coldfield—Stirling.
Newton-le-Willows—Stirling.

Routes to Oban and the West

For Routes to Scotland by Rail, Road, and Sea, *see* foregoing pages.

Travelling in Western Scotland is noteworthy for the reason that, whatever route one takes, the journey is bound to be interesting; whether one hurries on by train or motor, or makes a more leisurely journey by boat or cycle or afoot, one is led invariably through beautiful scenery. Some trains have Observation Cars attached for its better enjoyment.

When the traveller from the south has reached Edinburgh or Glasgow, he is faced with the following choice of routes and means of transport—

By Road:
  (1) *via* Stirling, Callander, Lochearnhead, Crianlarich, Tyndrum, and Dalmally—about 87 miles, Stirling to Oban; or bear north at Tyndrum for Fort William and the far West. This is the most direct route for those crossing the Border by Carter Bar or Berwick, or going straight through to Stirling without touching either Edinburgh or Glasgow.
  (2) *via* Glasgow, Balloch, Loch Lomond (the road skirts the whole length of the Loch) and Crianlarich, thence as above. The disadvantage of Glasgow's busy streets is handsomely outweighed by the charms of the lovely road alongside Loch Lomond. Glasgow to Oban, 92 miles.
  (3) *via* Arrochar, at the head of Loch Long. Arrochar is reached from Glasgow *via* Dumbarton and Garelochhead, or *via* Tarbet, 2 miles away, on Loch Lomond. From Arrochar by "Rest and Be Thankful" to Glen Kinglas and Loch Fyne, which is followed to Inveraray (58 miles from Glasgow). Hence to Cladich, on Loch Awe, and so by the Pass of Brander to Oban (96 miles from Glasgow). The most beautiful route to Oban, though not the most direct.

By Bus:
  There is a daily motor-coach service between Glasgow and Fort William *via* Loch Lomond and Glencoe; also between Glasgow and Oban, *via* Loch Long, Loch Lomond, and Crianlarich.

By Rail:
  (1) From Glasgow by the West Highland line *via* Dumbarton, the Gare Loch and Loch Long to Arrochar, and thence alongside Loch Lomond to Crianlarich, as Road Route (2), and continuing for Bridge of Orchy, and Fort William, or changing stations at Crianlarich for Oban.

By Steamer:
  (1) From Glasgow (daily service, except Sundays) to Ardrishaig and thence by motor-coach to Oban.
  (2) Craigendoran or Gourock to Inveraray by steamer; thence by road (*see* p. 23).

I.—TO OBAN *via* CALLANDER AND LOCHEARNHEAD

Approaching Stirling from the south, whether by road or rail, one passes the field of **Bannockburn**, where the Scots sealed the independence of their country (1314). A mile or so farther is **Stirling**, a spot brimful of historic interest. The castle was for centuries a favourite royal residence. Across the strath is the lofty Wallace Monument.

Note.—Motorists with time to spare can visit the **Trossachs** *en route* by taking the Aberfoyle road from Stirling and from Aberfoyle crossing over to the Trossachs, entered about a mile from Loch Katrine pier. From the pier turn back eastwards (by A821) till the main road (A84) is joined near the Pass of Leny.

The direct road from Stirling to Callander passes through **Bridge of Allan,** a popular inland resort, like **Dunblane,** 3 miles farther, which has a fine Cathedral. **Doune,** a pretty village 4 miles from Dunblane, has an ancient castle, introduced in Scott's *Waverley.* Then comes **Callander** (*see* p. 64), 8 miles farther; from here coaches run to the Trossachs.

From Callander, by the **Pass of Leny,** we reach **Loch Lubnaig,** in the State Forest of Strathyre, and so descend to pretty **Lochearnhead** (*hotels*), with charming views down Loch Earn. Then begins the long climb through gloomy **Glen Ogle,** a wild rocky valley, the watershed being crossed nearly a thousand feet above sea-level.

From Glen Ogle we descend into **Glen Dochart,** and our course is westward. On the south rises *Ben More*, with its twin *Stobinian*, respectively 3,843 feet and 3,827 feet in height. We follow the river to **Loch Dochart,** where is an island with remains of an old castle of the Clan Campbell. **Crianlarich** (*hotel* and *Youth Hostel*), though small, boasts two railway stations; here the Oban line (Lower Station) runs under the West Highland line (Upper Station) for Fort William and Mallaig.

From Crianlarich the way continues through a fine tract of country called **Strathfillan,** and passes the scanty ruin of **St. Fillan's Chapel,** one of the oldest of British churches. A mile beyond is **Dalree,** or *Dal Righ* ("the King's Field"), where Bruce lost the famous Brooch of Lorne (p. 37). Just under 35 miles from Callander is **Tyndrum** (*tyne'-drum*). A short distance farther is **Clifton,** at the beginning of the magnificent highway to Glen-coe, Fort William and Inverness (pp. 115-23).

The Oban road (A85) continues westward down Glen Lochy, with increasingly fine views of **Cruachan,** especially from the vicinity of **Dalmally.** A short way beyond that village **Loch Awe** reveals its northern end, with the hoary ruins of Kilchurn Castle. The route skirts the cloven foot of the Loch and soon we go through the **Pass of Brander** to **Taynuilt.** A little beyond the village of **Connel** there is a glimpse of **Dunstaffnage,** the strong-hold of the Scots kings over a thousand years ago. Then comes a descent and a sudden view of **Oban.**

II.—TO OBAN *via* LOCH LOMOND

Railway travellers see only the northern part of Loch Lomond; but by way of compensation the route skirts the Gare Loch and Loch Long. The Glasgow-Oban bus (Alexander's) follows the route described below.

From Glasgow towards **Dumbarton,** with its castle-crowned rock, the way is almost entirely industrial, but as we turn north (by A82) up the Vale of Leven by Bonhill (seat of the Smolletts) and Alexandria to **Loch Lomond** the scenery improves. The road runs for some 20 miles along the "bonnie, bonnie banks" and provides a series of views of unending charm. The southern end of the Loch is wide and besprinkled with green, wooded islets, but beyond Luss the waterway narrows, the steep slopes of **Ben Lomond** (3,192 feet) rising almost sheer from the water on the far side. At Tarbet a road runs off to Arrochar, on Loch Long (*see* Route III). Some 3 miles north of Tarbet a village has sprung up at Inveruglas in connection with the Loch Sloy Hydro-Electric Scheme, among the largest of its kind in Britain. A road has been built from Inveruglas to **Loch Sloy,** a lonely loch hemmed in by Ben Vane and Ben Vorlich, with a dam 1,160 feet long and 165 feet high. On the opposite shore from Inveruglas is Inversnaid, an important point on the Trossachs tour. At the head of Loch Lomond is **Ardlui,** whence by Glen Falloch we soon reach **Crianlarich** (51 miles from Glasgow, 41 from Oban). Thereafter the route is the same as Route I, p. 20.

III.—TO OBAN BY ARROCHAR AND INVERARAY

The railway serves this route only as far as Arrochar, then crosses to Loch Lomond and follows Route II. Buses run daily from Glasgow to Inveraray (*en route* for Ardrishaig and Campbeltown). MacBrayne's morning bus connects at Lochgilphead with their bus to Oban.

Having passed Dumbarton, **Craigendoran** and **Helensburgh,** road and railway closely follow the Gare Loch, an arm of the Firth of Clyde. On the right are the Luss Hills and the "Glen of Sorrow," as Glen Fruin is called, where, in 1603, the Colquhouns were slaughtered by the fierce Macgregors. The Gare Loch was a centre of activity during World War II and at Faslane Bay was constructed an important emergency port—now used for ship-breaking. **Garelochhead** (30 miles) is a pretty village built round the head of this narrow inlet. Crossing the neck of land at Whistlefield, we approach the eastern side of **Loch Long,** where at Finnart is a jetty for giant oil tankers—with storage tanks and a pipeline (57 miles) to the refineries at Grangemouth. The loch is 16½ miles from end to end. The mountainous district on its western shore, ironically termed Argyll's Bowling Green, forms the northern portion of the **Argyll National Forest Park.** The mountains here provide first-class opportunities for rock-climbers. On the lower ground are plantations of the Forestry Commission. Ben Arthur (2,891 ft.), popularly known as The Cobbler, is easily picked out with its distinctive outline.

From **Arrochar** the West Highland line and the road to Crianlarich cut over the low narrow ridge (only 1½ miles wide) which here separates Loch Long from Loch Lomond, Arrochar and Tarbet sharing a midway railway station. The Inveraray road (A83) keeps on round the head of Loch Long, passing the Succoth public camping ground (mouth of Glen Loin) and a torpedo-testing establishment. At **Ardgartan,** where the Croe Water enters the Loch, are extensive camp sites (with car park) and a Youth Hostel. Here the soft beauty of Loch Long is left as the road turns into wild and rugged **Glen Croe,** up which it climbs, reaching over 800 feet in 4 miles, with the jagged Cobbler on the right. The Glen ends at the col appropriately entitled "Rest and Be Thankful." Though the gradients have been eased and the hairpin bend at the summit has been eliminated, the ascent is testing, but the view is ample reward.

The road then descends beside Loch Restil and the falls below it to the bridge at the head of **Glen Kinglas.** A rather uncomfortable series of undulations leads down sharply to **Cairndow,** on the shore of Loch Fyne. From Cairndow the road proceeds to round the head of **Loch Fyne,** one of the longest (42 miles) of the narrow arms of the sea which penetrate this western coast and add charm as well as miles to road routes. The turreted tower of *Dundarave Castle,* close to the shore, is the "Doom Castle" of the novelist, Neil Munro. A mile or two beyond Dundarave **Inveraray** springs into view across the water; but to reach it the road has first to round the inlet from Loch Fyne known as **Loch Shira**—Glen Shira is the scene of a hydro-electric scheme. North of the town is the wooded hill of Duniquoich, a favourite view-point, and then, on the west bank of the Aray River, **Inveraray Castle,** the seat of the Duke of Argyll. Although the family have been settled here since the fifteenth century the present castle dates only from after 1745. Restored in 1953, the castle (with fine tapestries, portraits, arms, furniture, etc.) is open daily (except Friday) from Easter to September.

The county town (population 500) of Argyll, Inveraray (58 miles from Glasgow: 38 from Oban) was rebuilt in the eighteenth century. It has hotels (*George, McBride's*) and a Youth Hostel, a cinema and good fishing. A ferry (for foot passengers) crosses Loch Fyne to St. Catherine's. A steamer goes up Loch Fyne to Inveraray once or twice weekly in summer from Gourock *via* the Kyles of Bute.

From Inveraray the way to Oban is northward (by A819) through **Glen Aray,** well wooded and clothed with purple heath and golden broom. High up on the west side of the Glen, on a hill called Creag Dubh, is a monument to Neil Munro (1864-1930), who was born in Inveraray. The Aray has some fine falls and salmon pools.

At **Tighnafead** we leave Glen Aray. From this point a climb of a mile brings us to the summit of the pass connecting Glen Aray with the basin of Loch Awe. It has an elevation of 675 feet, and affords a delightful view of **Loch Awe** and Cruachan. Here the devout used to kneel on first coming in sight of the sacred island of Inishail. Two miles farther is the picturesque village of **Cladich,** near Loch Awe, with a road running up the loch to Ford.

23

The road to Oban proceeds northward along the eastern side of the loch to join Route I (A85) over a mile west of Dalmally. **Kilchurn Castle,** on a peninsula at the end of the loch, is one of the grandest baronial ruins in Scotland (*see* p. 56).

An alternative, though roundabout, way of reaching Oban from Inveraray is to continue (on A83) down Loch Fyne by Furnace and Crarae (with their granite quarries) to Lochgilphead (25 miles) and then proceeding north as in Route IV. Kilmory Castle, near Lochgilphead, is a Holiday Home for Youth Club members—thanks to the South African Aid to Britain Fund.

IV.—TO OBAN *via* ARDRISHAIG

Steamer to Ardrishaig (about 52 miles), thence to Oban (39 miles) by motor-coach (MacBrayne). Daily (except Sundays); from mid-September to mid-June the steamer turns at Tarbert, whence the journey to Oban is continued by motor-coach.

This is one of the most popular routes to Oban. The steamer leaves Gourock at 9.30 a.m. (connecting trains from Edinburgh and Glasgow). The steamer is due at Ardrishaig at 12.55 p.m.

Steaming across from **Gourock** to Dunoon, a distance of about 5 miles, we enjoy on a fine day a prospect scarcely equalled in Britain. In front is the Cowal shore, with its magnificent background of hills. On our right we have a fine view of **Loch Long,** stretching away northwards, with the pleasant summer resorts of **Kilcreggan** and **Cove** on one side and **Strone** and **Blairmore** on the other. The shorter and smaller inlet to the south of Loch Long is the now famous **Holy Loch.** The mansion on the height at **Strone Point,** between Loch Long and the Holy Loch, is Dunselma, long the residence of one of the Coats family, and now a Youth Hostel in the Argyll National Forest Park.

On the left, when the **Cloch Point** with its lighthouse is passed, a far-reaching stretch of the Renfrewshire and Ayrshire coast is disclosed. Away to the south, over the extensive waters, Bute, the Cumbraes and the gaunt peaks of Arran are seen.

Dunoon, the first place of call, is one of the most attractive and central seaside resorts on the Firth of Clyde. Here the Cowal Highland Gathering is held in August. Nearly opposite the next place of call, **Innellan,** is Wemyss Bay, beyond which Skelmorlie and Largs are visible on the Ayrshire side. Beyond Innellan is **Toward Point,** with a lighthouse. We now head to westward, making for Rothesay Bay, and with grand views of **Loch Striven,** which stretches northward for 9 miles amid lonely hills.

Celebrated in song and in history, **Rothesay,** which is the chief town in the Isle of Bute, enjoys a popularity of its own among Clyde holiday resorts. Its ruined castle dates from the early thirteenth century. From 1398 the eldest son of the Scottish sovereign bore the title of Duke of Rothesay. Now we head northward, and beyond Ardbeg Point pass **Kames Bay,** round which the village of **Port Bannatyne,** practically a continuation of Rothesay, ranges itself in crescent form.

Continuing our north-west course, we enter **The Kyles of Bute** and are amid the most enchanting scenery of the Firth of Clyde. The word Kyle, of Gaelic origin, means a narrow passage or strait. These particular "Kyles" are from half a mile to a mile in width. The northern end is the more picturesque. Shortly before reaching the mouth of Loch Riddon, we pass **Colintraive.** At this part of the Kyles of Bute graziers used to swim their cattle across from the mainland, on their return from the Argyllshire markets, and hence arose the name of Colintraive, which means the "swimming narrows."

After leaving Colintraive, the little islands that dot the channel seem every few minutes as if they would bar all further progress. **Eilean Dheirg,** or Red Island, is the small island on the east side of Loch Riddon about a mile from the entrance. It was in vain selected as his chief place of arms by Archibald, ninth Earl of Argyll, in his unfortunate rising with the Duke of Monmouth, in 1685.

Soon after this we touch at **Tighnabruaich,** which signifies in Gaelic "the house on the brae." It is a delightful seaside retreat with hotels and a Youth Hostel.

Having passed **Kames Pier,** we skirt the west, or Cowal, shore for about 5 miles, till abreast of **Ardlamont Point,** nearly opposite which is Ettrick Bay, in Bute. Rounding Ardlamont Point, we enter **Loch Fyne,** the longest of the many arms of the Firth of Clyde. Stretching far up into the heart of Argyllshire, this loch affords a clear run of 36 miles to Inveraray, or of 42 to its northern extremity. Loch Fyne is famous for its herrings.

After calling at **Tarbert** (*see* p. 49), we enter **Loch Gilp,** an inlet of Loch Fyne, with its port, Ardrishaig, and Lochgilphead, which are about a mile apart. At **Ardrishaig** (the "height full of briars") the outward voyage of the steamer ends, and passengers for Oban and the north land and proceed to Oban (some 40 miles) by motor-coach instead of by canal boat and steamer from Crinan as in old Royal Route days (*see* p. 48). Beyond Lochgilp-head the road leaves the canal side at Cairnbaan and runs north-wards, by Kilmartin, through country rich in relics of ancient history. The road is described (in the reverse direction) on p. 47.

V.—TO FORT WILLIAM BY GLENCOE

This magnificent road (part of A82) leaves the Oban road at **Clifton** (*see* Route I, p. 21), on the western edge of Tyndrum. Proceeding almost due north, it crosses from Perthshire into Argyll at a height of 1,033 feet, and then runs down the west side of the glen containing the railway to **Bridge of Orchy.** The road now keeps to the east of Loch Tulla (not going, as of old, by Inveroran and the west end of the loch) and climbs the hills to the north of Achallader to a height of 1,036 feet. After a short descent the road turns to the north-west, passes between Lochan na h-Achlaise and Loch Ba and rises to round the north-east shoulder of Beinn Chaorach at the height of 1,143 feet, its highest point. The road then makes for **Kingshouse,** but passes a quarter of a mile to the west of the hotel, crosses the River Etive, and follows the north side of the River Coupal to the watershed at the east end of **Glencoe** (1,024 feet). The descent into Glencoe is rapid and the road forces its way through the river gorge below the Study and then slants down the north side of the Glen to Loch Achtriochtan. The River Coe is crossed at the west end of that loch and the road thereafter follows the south side of the valley to Glencoe village and Carnach, where it joins the Balla-chulish-Kinlochleven road.

The total length of the "New" Glencoe road (Tyndrum to Carnach) is about 31 miles.

From the foot of Glencoe either the Ballachulish ferry (4 miles west; *see* p. 95) or the road round Loch Leven may be taken *via* Kinlochleven to Onich, whence the road skirts the south-eastern shore of Loch Linnhe all the way to Fort William.

VI.—ROAD ROUTES TO SKYE

The ferry linking Skye with the mainland crosses from **Kyle of Lochalsh,** which is reached by roads leaving the Great Glen at Invergarry and Invermoriston, joining at *Loch Cluanie* (*see* pp. 117 and 120).

Another route to Kyle of Lochalsh (in the main that followed by the railway) runs westward from Inverness to Garve, Achnasheen and Strome Ferry; but the ferry has to be used in order to cross Loch Carron and reach Kyle of Lochalsh.

For the Skye ferry, *see* p. 129.

Skye (Armadale) may also be reached by road or rail to **Mallaig,** and thence by steamer (*see* pp. 113-14, 129).

Inveraray Castle

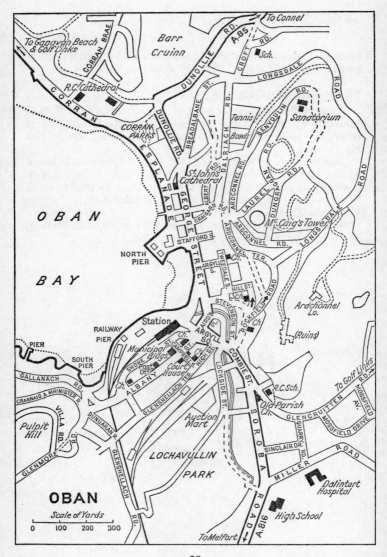

OBAN

Scale of Yards

0   100   200   300

Oban

Accommodation.—From Easter to October visitors have a choice of over a dozen licensed hotels and many (usually smaller and cheaper) unlicensed hotels, besides innumerable Board Residences and Apartments, a list of which may be obtained on application to the Information Bureau, Municipal Buildings. The larger hotels—several with about 100 rooms—are all situated on or near the Esplanade or Sea-front. These include—*Royal, Great Western, Caledonian, Alexandra, Marine, Esplanade, Park, Regent, Argyll, Rannachan, Lancaster, Columba, King's Arms, Balmoral, Clarendon.* Unlicensed hotels (with 10 or more rooms) are—*Corriemar, Achnamara, Barriemore*—all on the Esplanade; *Palace, Atholl*—in George Street.

Angling.—Loch Nell (boats for hire) has salmon and sea-trout from June after flood. Loch Awe, Loch Etive, etc., are within easy reach. A list of facilities in the district is available from the Information Bureau.

Banks.—*Bank of Scotland*, George Street; *British Linen*, opp. station; *Clydesdale and North of Scotland*, Argyll Square; *Commercial*, Argyll Square; *National*, George Street; *Royal Bank of Scotland*, George Street; *Union*, George Street; *Savings*, Argyll Square.

Bathing.—Sandy beach (with bathing boxes, safety equipment, and refreshment room) at Ganavan Bay (2 miles north of Oban). Service of buses and motor-boats from the Esplanade.

Boating and Yachting.—The Bay, sheltered by Kerrera Island, offers exceptional opportunities for safe boating. Motor-boats may be hired. With excellent anchorage and splendid cruising fields, Oban is one of the leading yachting centres in the country and its Regattas have a beautiful setting (*see* p. 32).

Bowls.—Green in Dalriach Road.

Buses to Dunollie and Ganavan; to Ardrishaig; to Kilmore, Kilninver and Easdale; to Connel and Taynuilt; and to Glasgow. A bus (Longsdale Road-Mossfield) links the north and south ends of the town. Oban is a good centre for motor-coach excursions.

Caravan site.—At Ganavan.

Cinema.—*Phoenix*, George Street.

Distances.—*By road.*—Ardrishaig, 39 miles; Ballachulish Ferry, 36; Easdale, 16; Edinburgh (*via* Callander) 122; Fort William (*via* coast and Ballachulish Ferry) 48, (*via* Kinlochleven) 67, (*via* Clifton, Glencoe and Kinlochleven) 94; Glasgow (*via* Inveraray and Arrochar) 96, (*via* Crianlarich and Loch Lomond) 92; Loch Awe Pier, 22; Taychreggan, 20.

By Rail.—Connel, 6; Loch Awe, 22; Killin (Loch Tay), 56; Callander, 70¾; Perth, 110; Aberdeen, 199¾; Glasgow (Buchanan Street), 117; Edinburgh, 123½; Manchester (Exchange), 328½; Liverpool (Lime Street), 330; Birmingham. 398½; London—Euston, 504; St. Pancras, 512½; King's Cross, 518¾.

By Steamer.—Fort William, 33; Tiree, 60; Tobermory, 30.

Early Closing.—Thursdays.

Fishing (Sea).—There are several good Fishing Banks in the neighbourhood, where whiting, codling, and gurnard can be caught from July to October. (Boat hirers will advise.)

Golf.—*Glencruitten* course, ½-mile from Oban Railway Station. 18 holes. Excellent club-house. Sunday play. At Ganavan are a short course and putting greens.

Hotels.—*Caledonian* (63 rooms) George Street; *Park* (75) Esplanade; *Great Western* (81) Esplanade; *Marine* (39) Esplanade; *Alexandra* (59) Esplanade; *Regent* (38) Esplanade; *King's Arms* (32) George Street; *Burnbank House* (10) Breadalbane Street; *Palace* (20, unl.) George Street; *Lancaster* (23,) Esplanade; *Crown*, *Lorn*, Stevenson Street; *Central*, Stafford Street; *Barriemore*, Esplanade; *Dunarle*, Esplanade; *Balmoral*, George Street, *Argyll*, Esplanade; *Columba*, North Pier; and many others of all categories.

Information Office.—Visitors' Information Bureau, Municipal Buildings, Albany Street.

Piers.—The principal is the *North Pier*, which occupies a central position in the bay. It is about 400 yards north of the Railway Station. On it is MacBrayne's Steam Packet Office. The *Railway Pier* adjoins the Railway Station. *South Pier*, and fish auction sales.

Places of Worship.—The usual hours of services on Sundays are 11 and 6.30; some churches have also a Gaelic service in the afternoon. *Church of Scotland.*—*Old Parish*, Combie Street; *St. Columba's Argyll*, Argyll Square; *Christ's Church*, Dunollie. *Baptist*, Albany Street; *Congregational*, Tweeddale Street; *Episcopal* (Cathedral Church of St. John), George Street; *Free Presbyterian*, Campbell Street; *Free High*, Rockfield Road; *Roman Catholic* (St. Columba's Cathedral), Corran Esplanade.

Population.—7,000.

Post Office.—Albany Street, near Station. Branches on Esplanade and in Soroba Road.

Railway Station.—A terminus of the Callander and Oban line of the Scottish Region of British Railways. The adjacent pier is used by all steamers running in connection with trains.

Tennis.—Hard courts in Dalriach Road, beside the Bowling-green.

Youth Hostel.—Hostel of Scottish Youth Hostels Association on Esplanade beyond R.C. Cathedral, with 100 beds.

Oban (pronounced *ō'ban*) is delightfully situated on the west coast of Scotland, in an almost land-locked bay. The town faces the green island of Kerrera and the lofty mountains of Mull and Morvern. The name is derived from the Gaelic equivalent of "a little bay."

Oban is one of the finest centres for those desiring to explore some of the wildest and most characteristic parts of Scotland. The excursions offered by the steamer and coach firms alone are almost bewildering in their variety; and those who also avail themselves of the railway, or who have their own car or cycle, will not readily exhaust the possibilities of the district.

The climate is mild, equable, and healthy. The myrtle, fuchsia, and other comparatively tender shrubs, live all the year round without protection, and the gardens and wild flowers afford indubitable evidence of the mildness of the climate. The snowfall in winter is very slight. The equability of temperature is mainly due to the proximity of the town to the warm ocean currents which wash the western coast of Scotland, to the prevalence of southerly and westerly winds, to the protection from easterly and northerly winds provided by the surrounding high hills and mountains, and to the shelter of the islands of Mull and Kerrera, which screen the town from Atlantic storms.

The first half of the year is the driest period. The last three months cover the wet season.

Oban is a parliamentary burgh, governed by a Council consisting of a Provost, two Bailies, and six Councillors.

Among the principal industries are the distillation of whisky and the manufacture of aerated waters and tweeds. Oban is at times a busy fishery centre, and has an important packing station for lobsters caught in Hebridean waters.

History

The site of Oban was occupied by man in prehistoric times. In 1888 a lake dwelling was discovered at Lochavullin, then a marshy tract at the southern end of the town. In 1894 a cave was found near the north end of George Street. It contained human skulls and the remains of various animals. Fish bones and shells were numerous and there were stone hammers and horn implements, harpoons, etc., ascribed to a period 3000 B.C.

In the latter half of the eighteenth century Oban was represented by a few thatched houses, whose occupants gained a living by fishing and farming. In 1791 houses began to increase around the clachan's "tolerable inn" of which both Dr. Johnson and Boswell speak in their diaries of their tour through the Highlands in 1773. Sir Walter Scott, when he visited Oban in 1814—his *Lord of the Isles* appeared the following year—described it as "a town of some consequence." During the first half of the nineteenth century the population rose from 600 to 1,500. It was not, however, till the application of steam as the motive power of the boats belonging to David Hutcheson, succeeded by David MacBrayne, that the town began to take its present position in the estimation of the travelling public, and the construction of the railway (1880) naturally made it a still more popular resort for holiday-makers. The *Oban Times*, a weekly, started in 1861, is the leading paper of the West Highlands.

The bay, being remarkably safe through the protection afforded by the Island of Kerrera, is a favourite yachting station. The West Highland Yachting Week is held at Oban in early August.

Besides the yachts of all sorts and sizes that may be seen in the season entering or leaving the bay or riding at anchor on its quiet waters, big liners and naval vessels are occasional visitors, and at all times there are steamers passing to and fro on one or other of the routes among the Western Highlands and Islands. Many a lonely lighthouse, too, is served by the Oban Station of the Northern Lighthouse Board.

It is during the **Oban Highland Games** week in late August that the bay and the town present their busiest and gayest aspect. During this Week is held the Argyllshire Highland Gathering, to which thousands flock. Throughout the season, however, Oban is never dull and between excursions delightful hours can be spent reposefully in admiring the glorious sunsets, feeding the swooping seagulls on the Esplanade or visiting a seal island in a motor-boat, listening to the Oban Pipe Band, attending a fish auction on the railway or South piers or a strenuous game of Shinty at Mossfield, enjoying a cup of tea in one of the restaurants, and studying the "souvenirs" in the shop windows or the flow of one's fellow tourists, so varied in garb and tongue.

The chief thoroughfare is **George Street,** which runs almost due north and south and with **Argyll Square** towards its southern extremity, hard by the railway station, forms the business part of the town. In the **Scottish Episcopal Cathedral of St. John the Divine,** at the north end of George Street, the reredos is a memorial of Bishop Chinnery-Haldane of Argyll and The Isles. St. Columba's Church, opposite, has been converted into offices of the Hydro-Electric Board since the congregation united with Argyll Square Church. The Free High Church, in Rockfield Road, behind Argyll Square, was designed by Augustus Pugin and won Ruskin's praise.

Northward of the steamer pier the bay is faced by the **Corran Esplanade,** with lovely views across the water that are particularly beautiful at sunset. Here are assembled many of Oban's leading hotels. In the Corran Parks is the new **Corran Hall** with restaurant and various social activities. Corran, in Gaelic, signifies a curved shore. **St. Columba's Roman Catholic Cathedral,** farther on, is a new all-granite building, designed by Sir Giles Scott. At the end of the Esplanade **The Plateau** begins, and the Ganavan Road leads along the shore past the 1914-18 War Memorial (the work of Alexander Carrick, R.S.A.) and Dunollie Castle to **Ganavan Sands,** Oban's "playground," in a delightful

bay, with bathing beach and golf links, a refreshment pavilion, a car park, and a popular caravan site. The motor road ends at Ganavan, but a farm road cuts over to the Oban–Connel road. Alongside the Esplanade sea-wall lie a number of motor-boats for hire. These motor-boats make frequent trips to neighbouring islets, where grey seals bask and have their nurseries.

Immediately behind the business portion of the town are **Oban Hill** and **Battery Hill,** which have their seaward sides dotted with private residences, while the summit of each is crowned by a structure that at once attracts attention. On Oban Hill is the skeleton of a huge hydropathic building (1880-1881) which had to be abandoned for want of funds. On the neighbouring height is a vast and even more conspicuous circular structure built of granite and bearing some resemblance to the Coliseum. It is known as **MacCaig's Tower,** from the name of its founder, a local banker who erected this "Folly" (in the last decade of the nineteenth century) as a personal and family memorial, and to aid unemployed masons.

The outlook from MacCaig's Tower richly repays the climber, but **Pulpit Hill,** less than half a mile south-west of the railway station, is generally considered the finest of the view-points of Oban. A useful mountain indicator at the top adds to the interest of the spot. The direct route from Argyll Square is along Shore Street—which fronted the beach before the construction of the railway—or up Albany Street, by the Municipal Buildings (which bear a plaque commemorating the visit of Queen Elizabeth in 1956—in an untimely downpour) and the Post Office. These thoroughfares unite just short of the bridge over the railway, which must be crossed, and then, straight ahead, is one of the footpaths leading up the hill. By following Crannaig a Mhinister Road and then doubling back cars can also reach the top.

The hill can be included in a circular walk of about 2 miles, approaching by Gallanach Road—which leads past the South Pier, the Lighthouse Pier, and the **Dungallan Public Parks,** facing Kerrera—and returning by Glenshellach Terrace and High Street.

Short Excursions from Oban

In addition to the excursions described in the following pages, steamers, motor-boats, and motor-coaches make trips to a number of places, concerning which notes will be found with the aid of the Index at the end of this book.

MacBrayne steamers make special day and evening excursions during the season (*see* handbills at North Pier).

British Railways offer a variety of circular tours; cheap day excursions to and from Oban; and Weekly Runabout tickets entitling holders to travel as often as they choose between Oban and Crianlarich, Bridge of Orchy, Spean Bridge and Fort William, and all intermediate stations.

1.—TO DUNOLLIE CASTLE

The Castle is undergoing repair and no admission particulars are available at the present time.

The Castle is an ancient relic in the northern outskirts of the town. It is approached by the Corran Esplanade and Ganavan Road and has the Maiden Island as an outpost.

Standing near the road, about a quarter of a mile from the Castle, is a huge upright, conglomerate pillar, or detached fragment of the rock known as plum-pudding stone. It is called *Clach-a-choin*, or the **Dog Stone,** from a tradition that Fingal, the great hero of Gaelic mythology, used it as a stake to which he bound his dog, Bran. Geologists attribute the stone and its abrasions to the action of the sea in remote ages when the coast was exposed to the open ocean.

"Nothing," says Sir Walter Scott, "can be more wildly beautiful than the situation of Dunollie." The ruins stand upon a bold promontory overhanging the Firth of Lorne. The principal part is the donjon or keep; but fragments of other buildings, overgrown with ivy, attest that it has been a place of importance.

These fragments enclose a courtyard, of which the keep probably formed one side, the entrance being by a steep ascent from the neck of the isthmus, formerly cut across by a moat, and defended, doubtless, by outworks and a drawbridge. Beneath the Castle stands the modern mansion of the Chief of the Clan MacDougall, with a garden (*private*) in which flourish bamboos and sub-tropical trees and plants of many kinds.

From the Ganavan Road by the foot of the Castle one gets a fine view across the Sound of Mull to the mountains of Mull and Morvern, and southward along Kerrera Sound to Easdale.

The earliest record of Dunollie Castle is in A.D. 685 and it was burned and rebuilt—probably of wood—several times between then and A.D. 733. The exact date of the present building is unknown, but is believed to be eleventh century. It was the principal seat of the MacDougalls, Lords of Lorne. The estate was forfeited in 1715, as its possessor had joined the Old Chevalier, but it was restored to the family for their loyalty in 1745. The word Lorne, or Lorn, by the way, is said to be derived from Loarn, the name of one of the leaders of the Scots, when they passed from Ireland to Argyll at the dawn of the sixth century. The territory to which his name became attached was his share of the spoil.

The MacDougall of Bruce's time married a daughter of the Red Comyn, whom Bruce slew before the high altar of the Greyfriars' Church at Dumfries, and sought by every means

36

vengeance for the death of his father-in-law. In 1306 he defeated Bruce at Dalree, near Tyndrum (*see* p. 20), and there secured—

> "The brooch of burning gold
> That clasps the chieftain's mantle-fold,
> Wrought and chased with rare device,
> Studded fair with gems of price."

For generations the brooch, actually of silver, was an heirloom of the family. It fell into the hands of Campbell of Bragleen when Gylen Castle, on the Island of Kerrera, was sacked and burned in 1647. It was restored to the MacDougalls in 1825 and is exhibited on rare occasions.

2.—TO GLENCRUITTEN

Glencruitten is a well-sheltered, green-mantled valley on the eastern side of the town. From Argyll Square it is approached by way of Combie Street, from which the left-hand branch at the Old Parish Church almost immediately enters the glen. A little to the right of the entrance is **Mossfield Park,** a spacious sports ground on which shinty, football, and other games are played.

On an eminence on the left side of the Glen is the West Highland Cottage Hospital, while on the face of the hill on the right runs the railway, at an exceptionally steep gradient. A short distance farther is the **Glencruitten Golf Course** (*see* p. 30).

The walk may be continued by the road leading northward to Connel, or southward to Loch Nell (*see* p. 40).

3.—TO GLENSHELLACH

This excursion is to the south and south-west of Oban. The route, which can be driven over, passes the site of *Lochavullin*, the Mill Loch—once an unsightly marsh, in which the remains of a prehistoric lake-dwelling were discovered when the tract was being reclaimed. It is now a fine playing field and car and bus park.

Not far within the pretty valley of **Glenshellach** is the McKelvie Hospital, near which urns of baked clay were unearthed in 1897. One contained a quantity of bones and charcoal, and a beautifully-shaped hammer-head of burnt clay with a glazed surface. About half-way along the glen, high up on the east side, stands

Soroba Lodge, once the residence of Robert Buchanan (1841-1901), poet and novelist, and also occupied by Sir George Trevelyan while editing the *Life and Letters* of his uncle, Lord Macaulay. The head of the glen is about 2¼ miles from Oban, and all along the road are charming prospects, including fine views (eastward) of Cruachan, and the Glen Etive mountains.

The homeward route (unless the sequestered track through Glenmore tempts the walker) is down the hill to the Gallanach Road, by the side of Kerrera Sound. (This road comes to an end a mile or so south at Gallanach estate. *En route* is Gallanach-more, the United Kingdom terminal of the first Transatlantic telephone cable.) On its way to Oban the road passes—not to mention an inviting tea garden—**Staffa Rock** (290 feet; *Ferry* to Kerrera), the **Ardbhan Craigs** (180 feet), the red stone castellated mansion called **Kilbowie Lodge** (County Educational Boys' Hostel), and what was once a carding mill worked by water power and overlooked by **Altnacraig,** long the Highland residence of Professor John Stuart Blackie (1809-1895). This versatile scholar forsook it when the railway reached Oban and the house was later occupied by the novelist and military historian, Ian Hay (Major-General John Hay Beith). Oban is entered by the **Dungallan Parks.**

4.—TO THE ISLAND OF KERRERA

Access.—By boat from the Esplanade, or by ferry from the Gallanach Road beyond Kilbowie Lodge (2 miles from Oban).

The Island of Kerrera (the accent is on the first syllable) lies west of the town, and makes Oban Harbour one of the safest and best in the kingdom. Kerrera is about 4 miles long and 2 broad. From its uplands there is a grand prospect of the mountains eastward, while seaward are some of the—

> "Hebrid Isles
> Placed far amid the melancholy main."

The view includes—

1. Northward—Lismore and the west coast of Loch Linnhe, the Morvern Hills. 2. Southward—The Island of Seil; farther off, the Isle of Scarba; and, still farther, the Paps of Jura. 3. South-west—The Isles of the Sea, and beyond them the sand knolls of Colonsay. 4. Westward—Mull, with Ben More (3,169 feet). 5. Eastward—Cruachan (3,689 feet).

The remnant of the ancient **Castle of Gylen** is the principal object of interest on the island. The route to it from the ferry landing-place is southward by road and path. Gylen was erected in 1587 as a stronghold of the MacDougalls of Lorne (*see* p. 36). The MacDougalls holding the castle for the King in the civil wars of the seventeenth century, it was destroyed in 1647 by a detachment of Leslie's army.

The highest point is **Kerrera Height** (617 feet), about half-way between the Ferry and the Castle; there is no defined path to it.

The island possesses historical interest from the fact that Alexander II died on it in 1249, while advancing against insurgent Western islanders. A hut was prepared for him in a field on Horse-shoe Bay still known as Dalry (the king's field), and his body was removed thence to Melrose Abbey for burial. In "The King's Field" is a spring bearing the name of the **King's Well**. Tradition says that Alexander drank of its water immediately before he expired.

In Horseshoe Bay King Haakon of Norway, with his fleet of galleys, took shelter on his way to decisive defeat at Largs (1263) at the hands of the Scottish King, Alexander III, who thereby added to his kingdom the Western Isles, held for centuries by the Norsemen.

At the north end of the island is an obelisk in memory of David Hutcheson, MacBrayne's predecessor (*see* p. 32).

5.—TO LOCH NELL

Oban to Loch Nell, 4¾ miles. The Easdale bus passes within a mile.

Leave Oban by Combie Street and Soroba Road, passing Oban High School and the Argyll Tweed Works. Soon will be seen high up on the right Soroba Lodge, Robert Buchanan's "white house on the hill" (*see* p. 37).

The road reaches its highest point about 2½ miles from Oban, and an extensive landscape opens. On the right a branch road turns off to **Kilbride,** a mile to the south-west, with a ruined church, an old burial-ground, and a finely-carved Celtic cross dating from 1516.

Just over 3 miles Ben Lui may be seen through the trees. Then comes the entrance to Dunach House, on the right, and a view of a portion of **Loch Feochan,** an arm of the sea, terminating in a lovely glen, watered by a boisterous mountain stream of the same name. At the foot of the hill a road turns sharp back on the left for *Cleigh*, just beyond which the road to Connel *via* freshwater Loch Nell, strikes up to the left.

Loch Nell, "Loch of the Swans," is nearly 2 miles long and half a mile wide. On each side are low hills, and the shores are in parts thickly wooded. The best view is obtained from the **Serpent Mound,** on the western side, about a quarter of a mile from the spot at which the loch is reached. The mound is formed of boulders and is supposed to be a relic of serpent worship. It is some 80 yards in length, and in the form of an elongated letter S. About 100 yards south of the mound is a cromlech, of which only the top stone is visible from a distance. According to local tradition, it marks the grave of the Ossianic hero, Cuchullin. The views are lovely all along the road.

Beyond the loch a minor road goes off up Glen Lonan on the right for Taynuilt. At the next fork the road to the right leads to Connel: that to Oban swings sharp to the left and shortly descends through Glencruitten.

6.—TO DUNSTAFFNAGE CASTLE

Bus services to the new village of Dunbeg, on Dunstaffnage Bay (3 or 4 miles from Oban on the road to Connel). Visitors may drive to within a quarter of a mile of the castle and walk the remainder of the distance. The castle and chapel may be visited during presence of workmen on Mondays to Fridays.

Dunstaffnage Castle is about a mile from the main road, the attractive eighteenth-century Dunstaffnage Mains, the home farm, being passed *en route*. The ruins stand on a narrow wooded peninsula at the entrance to Loch Etive from Loch Linnhe. Here, in the mid-thirteenth century, when the Norsemen were being ousted from Western Scotland, Ewen de Ergadia, a descendant of Somerled, King of the Isles, built a stronghold, whose name is probably derived from Celtic *dun*, fort, and

Norse *staffness*, staff point. Bruce besieged and captured it from the Lord of Lorne in 1308 (*see* p. 57) and later made a Campbell its Constable. To this day the Duke of Argyll is hereditary Keeper and Campbell of Dunstaffnage its hereditary Captain. The Castle was garrisoned by English troops during the Commonwealth and by the Campbells during the Jacobite Risings of 1715 and 1745. Flora Macdonald (*see* p. 142) was confined within its walls for a few days on her way to London as a state prisoner. From 1810, when a great fire destroyed the habitable portion of Dunstaffnage, the Captain took up his abode in Dunstaffnage House, over a mile to the east, which was also destroyed by fire in 1941, valuable relics being lost. A new house (1962) has been built on the site.

The ruins occupy a rocky site by the shore, with great curtain walls, 10 feet thick, 60 feet high and over 400 feet in perimeter. In plan the Castle is roughly quadrangular, with a round tower at each end of its north front. These curtains and towers, though altered at various times, "represent in substance the original Castle of the thirteenth century and form one of the best preserved and most interesting examples of its kind in Scotland." (*Dunstaffnage Castle* by Dr. Douglas Simpson.) The entrance is at the south-east corner, the Gatehouse (restored) being reached by a stone staircase (comparatively modern; originally a drawbridge). In the courtyard is a well or cistern, in front of a derelict eighteenth-century house.

Near the Castle, to the south-west, are the remains of a beautiful little ancient Chapel, beside which is the burial ground of the Campbells of Dunstaffnage. Some of the early Scottish kings are said to rest in a vault below the Chapel and it has been claimed that Dunstaffnage was a seat of the Dalriadic Scots and the repository of the *Stone of Destiny*—the legendary Pillow of Jacob or of St. Columba—before its transfer to Scone for the coronation (A.D. 844) of Kenneth MacAlpin, first king of the united Picts and Scots. From Scone the Stone was sent to England by Edward I in 1296 and has since formed part of the Coronation Chair at Westminster Abbey.

7.—TO CONNEL AND THE FALLS OF LORA

Three roads connect Oban and Connel. By using one for the outward journey and another for the return, those who are equal to a 10-mile walk (or longer) can have a very enjoyable circular excursion. The walk may, of course, be halved by taking train or bus to or from Connel. By the main road (A85) the sea is more in view. It climbs out of the town at the north end by Dunollie Road, passing Pennyfuir Cemetery and Lochan Dubh a couple of miles out. The other roads, rather less used by motorists, are attractive for walkers by their seclusion and rural charm. Both turn off the Glencruitten road, the middle road leaving it a mile and a "bittock" from Oban and keeping just west of the railway line to join the main road near Dunstaffnage House, while the Old Road, considerably longer, continues eastward for over a mile before branching north and running down beside the Lusragan Burn to Connel Bridge.

Connel (*Falls of Lora, Dunstaffnage Arms*; unl. *Craiglora*) is an attractive little village with hotels and other accommodation for visitors, grand views, boating, fishing, and numerous walks and excursions. There is a frequent bus service to Oban and northwards to Kinlochleven, and buses also run to Taynuilt. St. Oran's Church is built after the style of Iona Cathedral. There is also a small Episcopalian church.

The bridge over the mouth of Loch Etive gives access on to the Ballachulish road.

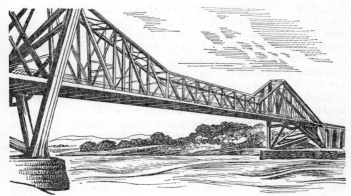

Connel Bridge

Just east of the bridge are the **Falls of Lora,** not ordinary falls but remarkable two-way salt-water rapids. As the tide ebbs or flows the waters of Loch Etive—a good example of an ancient submerged glen—surge noisily out or in over a barrier ridge covered at high tide. Lora is frequently mentioned in the Ossianic poems—"The murmur of thy streams, O Lora, brings back the memory of the past." Connel derives from Comhal, father of Fingal.

It was in 1730 that James Macpherson published *Fragments of Ancient Poetry* and followed this book with "Translations of *Fingal* and *Temora*," poems, which he attributed to an ancient bard, Ossian. Dr. Johnson challenged the authenticity of the poems in characteristic manner, and controversy became hot. The final blow was struck when a subscription was raised to print the originals, and no originals were forthcoming. Nonetheless, Ossian enjoyed an amazing vogue, abroad as well as at home.

8.—TO BARCALDINE CASTLE, GLEN SALACH AND ARDCHATTAN PRIORY

Distance.—From Oban by Connel bridge to Barcaldine Castle, 4½ miles.
Motorists.—The road (A828) may be followed northward from Barcaldine House and along the shores of Loch Linnhe to Ballachulish. The return could be made by Glencoe, *see* p. 71.

From the north end of Connel Bridge (*Loch Nell Arms*; *see* p. 42) a level road runs across the **Ledaig** or **Moss of Achnacree,**

43

supposed to be Ossian's "Plains of Lora." It is notable as the site of an ancient lake-dwelling and for the remains of a cairn said to mark the burial-place of the Gaelic Homer. (Large caravan club site at North Ledaig). Daily flights are operated by *Loganair* from a nearby airstrip.

Rather more than 2 miles from Loch Etive, commanded on the east by Beinn Lora (1,007 feet), is the village of **Benderloch,** a charming place for a quiet holiday, with fishing, bathing, walking, camping, etc. The eminence beside the village is *Beregonium*, reputed to be the site of the capital of the Fingalian kings and the Dalriadic Scots. The view from the summit is superb: it includes Tralee Sands, extending westward towards Loch Nell Castle, Lady Margaret's Tower on the wooded promontory across Ardmucknish Bay (the salt-water Loch Nell), Kerrera, and Mull. There are remains of prehistoric fortifications on Beregonium, which, as Dun MacUisneachan, figures in the old Celtic legend, *Tale of the Sons of Uisnach*. Where the boats lie on the pebbly beach at its base is **Port Selma,** and the locality around has been identified as the Selma of the Ossianic poems.

Beyond Benderloch, the main road curves round north-eastwards, to make its way round Lock Creran, the entrance to which is almost blocked by the island of Eriska (*private*).

Prominently placed about 2 miles north of Benderloch, about a mile west of the main road, and at a short distance from the shore of Loch Creran, is **Barcaldine Castle**, the ancient seat of the Campbells of Barcaldine, cadets of the noble house of Breadalbane. This sixteenth-century "Black Castle" has been restored and whitewashed.

About 4 miles from Benderloch, as the road runs among fine beech trees, a narrow road on the right strikes south-east up Glen Salach to join up with the road running along the north side of Loch Etive and which ends opposite Bonawe. (For the route on to Ballachulish *see* pp. 69-70.)

Glen Salach

On the left of the glen is **Beinn Bhreac,** "the spotted mountain" (2,324 feet). The ascent through the glen continues for fully 3 miles. From the highest point, 516 feet, there is a steep descent of over a mile, giving a fine view of Loch Etive, and of the more distant Cruachan. When the road approaches the loch a turn right leads to **Ardchattan Priory** (*gardens open May-Oct.*), a religious house of the Valliscaulian Order, founded in 1231 by Duncan MacDougall, Lord of Lorne. In 1308 King Robert the Bruce assembled within its walls the last national council conducted in the Garlic tongue.

The ruined **Priory Church** (Ministry of Public Buildings and Works) is open for inspection. The chapel was burned by Cromwellian troops from Dunstaffnage in 1654, when the then Laird of Ardchattan supported Glencairn's rising against Cromwell. Within are the tombs of two priors, the grave of Colin Campbell, and other sculptural stones of interest.

Three miles east of Ardchattan are the large granite quarries opposite Bonawe. The former ferry here has ceased and the return to Connel is made back along the north shore of Loch Etive.

Ardchattan Priory

Longer Excursions—By Land

I.—TO EASDALE

Buses daily (16 miles); motor-coaches in the season. This is a favourite afternoon trip, with time for tea at Easdale.

The route for the first few miles is described on pp. 39-40 as the road to Loch Nell. Beyond the turning for Cleigh the road skirts the southern shore of the almost land-locked **Loch Feochan** to the little village of **Kilninver,** at the mouth of the *Euchar,* 8 miles from Oban. Here the road to Easdale bears to the right, climbing steeply, then dropping down to **Loch Seil** (with a lake-dwelling). At Achnasaul (11 miles) a road leads off south to Ardmaddy Castle, on the eastern shore of Seil Sound, which separates the island of **Seil** from the mainland. This strait is extremely narrow at its northern end, where it is crossed by **Clachan Bridge,** the so-called "Bridge over the Atlantic." This quaint single-arch structure of Telfer's is designed to let vessels pass under it.

After running down the west side of Seil Sound for a couple of miles we leave the Cuan Ferry road and cut across the island by Kilbride (scene of an old Gaelic College) to the white-washed cottages of Ellenabeich (*Inshaig Park Hotel*), off which lies **Easdale** island (*ferry*). Easdale gave its name to the roofing slates exported from all the neighbouring **Slate Isles**—Seil, Luing, Torsay, Shuna, etc. The slate quarries of this region were active for over 200 years till hit by changing fashion and disaster. In 1881 the sea broke in and flooded the largest of them, which had attained a depth of 300 feet. Quarrying continues at Balvicar and Cullipool on Luing. Their are some glorious views of mountains, sea, and islands, far and near.

Luing, which with Torsay and Shuna shields Loch Melfort from the west, is reached by **Cuan Ferry** (cars carried: bus from Oban) at the southern tip of Seil Island. At **Cullipool,** on the north-west coast of Luing, is a vast lobster storage pond formed by concrete blocks and slate stone dams—the first sea-water pond of the kind in the kingdom. Some 40,000 lobsters are kept here, fed daily, and supplied to British and Continental markets.

II.—TO CRINAN, ARDRISHAIG AND KINTYRE

In the season there are motor-coach tours from Oban to Crinan and Tayvallich, on Loch Sween, and shorter afternoon tours to Melfort. All the year round MacBrayne de luxe coaches run daily (except Sundays) between Oban and Ardrishaig, connecting there with the mail steamer (*see* p. 24). On certain days in summer one can sail down Loch Fyne by steamer, pass through the Kyles of Bute, land at Dunoon, and return thence to Oban by coach *via* Inveraray, a delightfully varied round trip.

As far as Kilninver (8 miles south of Oban) the route is the same as that to Easdale, described on p. 46. At Kilninver the road to Ardrishaig (A816) turns off at right angles and climbs up pretty Glen Euchar for a couple of miles. Proceeding through wooded, steep-sided Glen Gallain, it then follows the *Oude*—involved with Loch Tralaig to the east in a hydro-electric scheme—down to the **Pass of Melfort** (14 miles from Oban), one of the most picturesque parts of the Western Highlands. Here, where the river flows in a deep and beautiful ravine, the old road had to be closed to vehicular traffic owing to the danger of loose and overhanging rocks and now the highway goes over a hill above the Pass, commanding a magnificent view.

Beyond the Pass, at **Kilmelfort** (16 miles), in charmingly laid-out grounds, is the *Cuilfail Hotel*, well known to anglers. (Guests have a choice of lochs, with boats provided; these include Loch Avich, 5 miles to the east, reached by a hilly road leading over to Loch Awe and Taychreggan, *see* p. 53).

After skirting the southern shore of **Loch Melfort**, an arm of the sea 4 miles long and 2 miles wide, shut off from the Firth of Lorne by Luing, Shuna, and other islands (*see* p. 94), we cut across to **Kintraw** (24 miles) at the head of another romantic inlet, **Loch Craignish.** Many an islet breaks its surface and its western shore tapers to a Point opposite the tip of Jura, where tidal currents race. Craignish Castle, near the Point, defied "Colkitto" and his wild Irishmen in the mid-seventeenth century.

Up the narrow Pass of Kintraw the road climbs steeply to over 500 feet, then plunges downward to **Kilmartin** (30 miles), passing the roofless **Carnasserie Castle,** which was burned as a Campbell property during Argyll's rebellion in 1685. Carnasserie was the seat of the last Bishop of the Isles and Abbot of Iona, John Carswell, author of the first book printed in Gaelic, a translation (1567) of Knox's "Liturgy." Kilmartin has two fine crosses in its churchyard. It lies in the heart of a glamorous region, rich in relics of Dalriada (*c*. A.D. 500), the nucleus of the Kingdom of the Scots. Numerous cairns to the south and west of Kilmartin bear Bronze Age cup-and-ring markings on the rock surface. **Dunadd** hill fort, the capital of Dalriada, lies east of the road, near Kilmichael Glassary, as we approach Bridgend (34 miles), and is likewise in the safe-keeping of the Ministry of Works as an Ancient Monument.

A mile beyond Kilmartin the direct road to Crinan leaves the Ardrishaig road, which meets the Canal at **Cairnbaan** (*hotel*). From Cairnbaan one can follow the canal westwards to Bellanoch, 2 miles short of Crinan, and then turn south for **Loch Sween,** the sea loch near whose head is the inviting village of **Tayvallich** (about 40 miles from Oban). Another favourite picnic spot, **Carsaig Bay,** on the Sound of Jura, is close at hand. Crinan village (*hotel*), at the western end of the Canal, is beautifully situated on Loch Crinan and offers good boating and fishing. To the north **Duntroon Castle** imposingly commands the entrance to the Loch. Since the withdrawal of the Crinan Canal steamers from the Glasgow-Ardrishaig route to and from Oban, this lovely little corner of Scotland has undeservedly been rather side-tracked.

The Crinan Canal.—The Canal was cut to afford direct and safe communication between the West Coast and Isles on the one hand and Loch Fyne and the Firth of Clyde on the other, and to avoid the circuitous and often rough passage of 70 miles round the Mull of Kintyre. Begun in 1793, opened in an incomplete state in 1801 and finished in 1817, the Canal is 9 miles long and for many years it formed a picturesque part of the Royal Route to Oban—so called after Queen Victoria followed it in 1847. The numerous locks—there are fifteen of these—inevitably made for slow progress, so much so that passengers were wont to land from the small canal vessel and walk part of the way to Crinan, where another steamer awaited them for the completion of the voyage. Nowadays MacBrayne motor-coaches carry passengers from Ardrishaig to Oban in the time—a couple of hours—it took the boat to pass through the Canal.

The main road continues southwards from Cairnbaan and joins the Inveraray-Campbeltown road (A83) near Lochgilphead (*Argyll, Stag*), whence we pass along the shore of Loch Gilp for a couple of miles to **Ardrishaig** (40 miles: *Royal, Anchor,* unl. *Auchendarroch*). In the season Ardrishaig is the turning point of

Oban, from Pulpit Hill (*J. Salmon Ltd.*)

Kerrera, and Firth of Lorne (*J. Salmon Ltd*).

Ganavan Sands, Oban (*Valentine*)

Tobermory, Isle of Mull (*J. Salmon Ltd.*)

the daily mail steamer from Gourock (*see* p. 24), with motor-coach connection to and from Oban, **Tarbert**, 12 miles down Loch Fyne, taking its place for the rest of the year (October to April). The name Tarbert denotes an isthmus across which boats could be dragged (*cf.* Tarbet on Loch Lomond) and here a narrow slip of land links Knapdale to Kintyre and separates breezy Loch Fyne from the sheltered waters of **West Loch Tarbert,** from which steamers and car ferry ply to Islay, Jura and the smaller islands of Gigha and Colonsay. Herring may now fight shy of Loch Fyne, but not so tourists, for, like Ardrishaig, the little fishing village of Tarbert (population 1,650) is visited in summer by shoals of holiday-makers. Golf, boating, fishing, and a cinema are among its distractions.

The road to Campbeltown follows the southern shore of West Loch Tarbert and as the open sea is approached the island of Gigha appears and then from Clachan (23 miles from Ardrishaig: *Balinakill House Hotel*) Islay and Jura rise majestically from the ocean away to the west.

At **Tayinloan,** 8 miles south, Gigha is less than 3 miles distant and a ferry crosses to it. Thence to Campbeltown (50 miles from Ardrishaig) the chief interest lies in a succession of grand sea-views; on a reasonably clear day Rathlin Island and Fair Head, in Ireland, are visible. The last few miles take us across low-lying ground to **Campbeltown** on the east side of Kintyre. Campbeltown (population 6,500: *Argyll Arms*, *Royal*, *White Hart*, *Ardshiel*) has a well-preserved Iona Cross in its main street. Its harbour is at the head of a deep bay, opposite the southern end of Arran. Noted as a fishing port and for its distilleries, Campbeltown has no lack of entertainment for its visitors—a museum, cinemas, boating and angling, and famous golf links at **Machrihanish** (*Ugadale Arms*: unl. *Warren*), 6 miles away on the western side of Kintyre. Its air-port (Machrihanish) brings it within an hour's flight from Glasgow (Renfrew), with which city Campbeltown is also connected by bus.

From Campbeltown a road goes inland by Conie Glen to **Southend** (*Keil*, *Argyll Arms*), the most southerly village in Kintyre. Out to sea is lonely Sanda, with little Sheep Island in attendance. Westward, a rough track climbs over 1,000 feet and down precipitously to the lighthouse on the **Mull of Kintyre**, with a glorious outlook across the North Channel to Ireland.

Up the east coast of Kintyre runs a secondary road, with steep gradients and dangerous turns but with delightful views of Arran. **Saddell,** nearly 10 miles north of Campbeltown, has the ruins of a twelfth-century monastery. **Carradale** (*hotel*) offers good fishing and hill-climbing. On the shores of the bay is a vitrified fort and the ruins of Airds Castle overlook Kilbrennan Sound. Grogport (19 miles) has a quaint and inviting name. At Claonaig (28 miles) the road forks; one can continue 2 or 3 miles up the coast to **Skipness,** with a ruined castle and church of St. Columba, or cut across the peninsula to West Loch Tarbert and so reach Tarbert (38 miles) and Ardrishaig (50 miles).

From West Tarbert a winding road follows the northern shore of West Loch Tarbert and then strikes northward along the coast to Loch Killisport and so to Inverniel, a few miles south of Ardrishaig. Walkers who like to get off the beaten track can go west from the head of Loch Killisport by a rough and wild road and up the eastern shore of **Loch Sween**—past the ruins of Castle Sween, which dates from the early thirteenth century—to Bellanoch, on the Crinan Canal. Kilmory and Eilean Mor, a couple of miles off the coast, both have ancient chapels and sculptured stones of special interest.

ISLAY

From West Tarbert a MacBrayne steamer sails daily (except Sunday) to Islay in connection with the Glasgow-Ardrishaig boats. (Motor-coach from East to West Tarbert.) On Tuesday, Thursday, and Saturday it calls at Gigha on the way to Port Ellen in southern Islay; on Monday, Wednesday, and Friday it calls at Jura on the way to Port Askaig in eastern Islay, going on to Colonsay on Monday and (in summer) on Friday.

Local coach services operate on Islay and connect with Port Ellen and Port Askaig for steamers.

A twice-daily car ferry service is operated by Western Ferries Ltd. between Kennacraig, West Loch Tarbert, and Port Askaig, calling at Gigha (North End) and turning at Jura (Feolin).

Air service on weekdays from Abbotsinch.

Gigha (*gee*-ha: g hard), a small island off the west coast of Kintyre, is halfway in the three-hour passage from West Tarbert to Port Ellen. It has caves and sandy bays, charming wild flowers and fascinating antiquities, which include an ogham stone. The Reverend Dr. Kenneth MacLeod, writer of the song *The Road to the Isles*, was long the parish minister here.

Islay, biggest and most frequented of the southern group of Inner Hebrides, stretches north and south for some 25 miles and is almost 20 miles across at its widest. The population (about 3,900) is but a third of what it was a century ago. For holiday-makers the island presents excellent bathing and fishing and golf; it is noted for its Celtic Crosses; its atmosphere is soothing and peaceful, though it has a poignant reminder of war on the Mull of Oa in a Monument (erected by the American National Red Cross) to U.S.A. soldiers and sailors who perished in 1918 in the wrecks of the transports *Tuscania* (torpedoed) and *Otranto* (in collision) off the coast of the Rhinns, in the south-west.

Port Ellen, in the south-east, is the commercial capital, being the entrepôt for the extensive distillery concerns throughout the island. It has hotels (*White Hart, Islay*) and its links at **Machrie** (3 miles north-west: *hotel*) are beloved of golfers. Southward of Port Ellen the coast rises to the **Mull of Oa,** a superb viewpoint. A fine example of Islay's Celtic sculptured stones is Kildalton Cross (7 miles N.E.). Northward buses run by *Glenegedale Airport* to Bowmore (*Imperial, Seaview, Lochside*), a distilling village, with chief shops, and an ancient round church, on Loch Indaal, which penetrates far into the west coast. This road (A846) continues to Bridgend (*hotel*) and cuts right across the island to Port Askaig (22 miles from Port Ellen). From Bridgend another road goes down the west side of Loch Indaal to **Port Charlotte** (*hotel*) and to Portnahaven (*hotel*) at the south end of the Rhinns.

Port Askaig (*hotel*) is a link not only between Islay and the mainland but between Islay and Jura and Colonsay. A ferry crosses the narrow Sound of Islay to Feolin in Jura and a steamer serves Colonsay on certain days of the week.

Jura, unlike its neighbour, is aloof and unwelcoming. Its meagre population (under 300) is scattered and there is but one hotel. Rugged and mountainous, with its distinctive **Paps** rising to 2,500 feet in the Forest north of Feolin, the "deer isle" (Scandinavian *deor-oe*) is 28 miles long and in places 9 miles wide. A road runs round the south coast from Feolin Ferry and up the east side to Tarbert, where Loch Tarbert, on the west coast, almost divides Jura in two. Otherwise the island is more or less trackless. At the north end the Gulf of **Corryvreckan,** notorious for its whirlpool, separates Jura from the island of Scarba. Corryvreckan (*i.e.* Brecan's Cauldron) figures in ancient sagas and present-day films alike. The village of Craighouse, where the steamer calls, is well to the south, on the east coast, which is kindlier than the desolate west, the latter being marked by "raised beaches" and numerous caves.

Colonsay lies west of Jura. Its port, Scalasaig, has an hotel. The vegetation of Colonsay is remarkable, indicative of the mild climate. A sound 100 yards wide, dry at low tide, parts Colonsay from its tiny satellite **Oronsay,** on which are the ruins of a fourteenth-century Priory and a finely sculptured sixteenth-century cross. The islands take their names from St. Columba and his colleague St. Oran.

Loch Awe and hotel

III.—LOCH AWE

Third largest and one of the most beautiful of Scotland's many lochs, Loch Awe is 23 miles long and is narrow—less than ¾ mile except at its foot in the north. The maximum depth is 307 feet, about 5 miles from its head. The loch is surrounded by mountains, mostly between 1,000 and 2,000 feet in height, with Cruachan, twice as high, commanding the northern end. A great stretch of its western bank and patches of its eastern side are forested. Romantic islands adorn its surface. Geologists tell us that originally Loch Awe's surplus waters flowed from its southern end into the Sound of Jura, instead of escaping down the river Awe to Loch Etive as they do now; this may account for the unusual feature that the head of the Loch is today tame in comparison with its foot.

In mediæval days the Loch Awe district was largely MacGregor country, but in the fifteenth century the Campbells obtained a footing and the shores and islands of the loch and the recesses of the neighbouring glens were for generations their retreat in time of danger. Their slogan, or war-cry—"It's a far cry to Lochow," *i.e.* Loch Awe—with which they derided their foes and indicated the impossibility of reaching them in their distant fastnesses, is said to have originated in the call of a Campbell girl heard from an incredible distance among the hills as she fled from her Macdougall husband. Another tale connects it with a remark of Campbell of Inverliver, on carrying away (1499) the red-haired little Muriel, heiress of Cawdor, in distant Nairnshire, to the protection of his chief here. "Suppose she should die?" said one of his men. Inverliver laughed and replied, "Muriel of Cawdor will never die as long as there is a red-haired lassie on the shores of Lochow."

Motor-boats ply in summer from one end of Loch Awe to the other. Loch Awe is a favourite anglers' rendezvous and the hotels scattered along its banks provide boats and gillies for guests attracted by its salmon and trout. (Rod fishing for salmon opens on February 12 and closes on October 15.)

The North of Scotland Hydro-Electric Board has, naturally, cast its eye on Loch Awe and its vast scheme includes a barrage (with a fish pass) across the Awe near its outflow from the Loch, with a tunnel conveying water to a power-station between Inverawe House and the river mouth on Loch Etive; an underground reversible pumping station three-quarters of a mile inside Ben Cruachan, with a storage reservoir high up the Allt Cruachan on the mountain-side; and a power-station at Inverinan, half-way along the western side of Loch Awe, fed by a tunnel from Loch Nant, itself enlarged by a dam.

From Oban, Loch Awe may be visited—

(*a*) By car to Ford along either the eastern or western shores. The round trip of the loch is about 80 miles.

(*b*) By motor-coach to Loch Awe (pier, hotel) at the northern end of the Loch (22 miles from Oban).

(*c*) By road to Taychreggan, on the west bank of the Loch—a daily afternoon coach trip from Oban.

(*d*) By train. The nearest station is Dalmally—3 miles from Loch Awe Hotel.

In circling Loch Awe the best approach, for scenic reasons, is by the more distant south end at Ford (31 miles from Oban). For most of this stage the route is the same (A816) as that to Ardrishaig (*see* p. 47). Near the ruined Carnasserie Castle (28 miles) the Loch Awe road (B840) turns sharply to the left and enters the **Pass of Craigenterive** (*Creagantairbh*). Dog's Head Loch, on the right, is said to owe its name to its appearance when viewed from neighbouring hills. The pretty lake beyond it is **Loch Ederline.** From **Ford** (*hotel*), an angler's resort, a road runs north for ¾ mile to the Pier. We, however, go eastward and hug the eastern shore of the loch for its entire length. Soon after reaching Loch Awe, we pass the haunted ruins of **Kilneuair Church,** which is mentioned in Argyll charters as far back as 1394. A mile further on stands **Fincharn Castle,** on a steep rock, a Macdonald stronghold of old. Opposite Braevallich (6 miles from Ford) is the deepest stretch of the loch (50 fathoms) off Innis Stiuire, an islet behind which the pioneer **State Forest of Inverliever** (between 12,000 and 13,000 acres) extends for 9 miles along the western bank, with a new village at Dalavich for its workers and those of Inverinan Forest adjoining it. **Portinnisherrich** (9 miles) looks across the loch to a solitary pier with the incongruous name of New York, near Dalavich. On Innis Sherrich (*Searamhach*) to the south is an old chapel; on Innis Chonnell to the north are the ivy-clad ruins of **Ardchonnell Castle,** once the chief seat of the Campbells.

A little way up the *Allt Blarghour*, which enters the loch a couple of miles past Portinnisherrich, are **Blairgour Falls,** 90 feet in height, reached by a path on the north bank of the burn. On the other side of Loch Awe the Avich leaps into the lake at the end of its short course from Loch Avich (*see* p. 60).

We now reach the lower half of Loch Awe, which is much grander in character, with Cruachan, a dozen miles away, making a noble background. The loch narrows on its way to **Portsonachan** (17½ miles from Ford: *hotel*: angling, deer-stalking). Here we go slightly inland to join the Inveraray road (A819) at **Cladich** (21 miles) after a sharp climb from **Ardbrecknish** (*hotel*: fishing, shooting). Crossing the *Allt an Stacain* at Cladich, we return to the lochside at **Inistrynich,** a beautiful peninsula which looks out upon the hallowed island of **Inishail,** "the isle of repose," one of the most fascinating of the many islands here gracing Loch Awe at its widest. At one time the site of a Cistercian nunnery, Inishail was for ages the burial ground of the various clans who held sway in this part of Argyll. The southern part of the green isle has the ruin of a chapel.

West of Inishail, on a promontory, stands the mansion-house of Ardanaiseig, and north of it a cluster of smaller islands guard the approach to the wide but tapering arm which the Loch stretches out along the Pass of Brander, towards Loch Etive. The first of these isles, **Fraoch Eilean** ("heather island") was so named, according to a Celtic tradition, after a gallant knight, the lover of the fair Gealchean. The girl's mother, Mai, also loved the hero and, that she might be a successful rival of her daughter, she bade Fraoch fetch from the island the apples of immortal youth, which were guarded by a dragon. Fraoch undertook the quest and slew the dragon, but died of the wounds he received, while Mai was poisoned by eating the fruit. In 1267 Alexander III gave the island to Sir Gilbert MacNaughton, on condition that he would entertain the Scottish monarch should he ever pass that way. Only fragments of the castle walls remain.

Between 2 and 3 miles beyond Cladich the old road makes straight for Dalmally, up past the high-perched **Duncan Ban McIntyre Monument.** This celebrated Gaelic poet (1724-1812) was Gamekeeper of Ben Doran. He could neither read nor write. **Dalmally** (27 miles from Ford; 25 miles from Oban) lies at the foot of Glen Orchy, among high hills and with delightful environs. The hotel has 6 miles of salmon fishing on the *Orchy*, among other attractions for the angler. A much-worn stone in front of it is known as "Bruce's Chair." The churchyard contains many ancient tombstones, while nearly opposite it is the Gallows Hill, on which the Clan Gregor hanged those condemned to death. By road (A85) or rail Dalmally is about 3 miles east of Loch Awe pier.

The main road down Loch Awe today by-passes Dalmally, keeping beside the loch to its northern extremity and joining the Oban road near the marshy peninsula on which stands defiantly the ruin of **Kilchurn Castle** (27 miles from Ford).

The oldest portion of Kilchurn (Kil-*hoorn*) is the tower, built in 1440 by Sir Colin Campbell, an ancestor of the Breadalbane family. Sir Colin (according to a traditional story) soon after left for a crusade in the Holy Land. When he had been seven years from home and his lady had heard nothing of him, a report reached the castle that he was slain in battle; and his supposed widow in due time accepted another suitor, MacCorquodale. The wedding-day was fixed, but on its morning the missing lord entered the castle in disguise. Amid the festivities preceding the celebration of the nuptials, he disclosed himself, to the great delight of his lady and his followers. The castle was greatly enlarged in 1693, and it continued to be a residence of the family till 1740. The ruin (in care of the Ministry of Works: admission free) shows a square tower surrounded by high walls, with battlements and round turrets.

On the northern side of the Kilchurn peninsula, the river *Orchy*, joined by the river *Strae*, enters the loch, about a mile north-east of Loch Awe pier.

Loch Awe (*Loch Awe, Carraig Thura*) is an admirable centre for angling, boating, climbing, and touring in all directions. At Easter, courses of instruction in casting, trolling, spinning, and the handling of boats are conducted by experts with local knowledge, the huge Loch Awe Hotel serving as base. For scaling nearby Cruachan this is a convenient starting or finishing point. So, too, for runs to Glencoe, Loch Tay, Loch Lomond, Inveraray, etc. Kilchurn Castle (*see* above) may be reached by boat from Loch Awe Pier, the distance being under a mile. The Loch itself can be explored by motor-boat or by road along the eastern side (*see* pp. 53-5).

Loch Awe Pier to Oban.—Both road and railway line skirt the northern shore of Loch Awe and the southern side of bulky **Cruachan** (3,689 feet). About a mile from the pier is **St. Conan's Kirk,** erected (1881-1930) on the site of an old church as a memorial to the Campbells of Blythswood and Innis Chonain and containing historical relics. **Innis Chonain,** the island nearest the shore, takes its name from St. Conan, patron saint of Lorne, a pupil of St. Columba. A couple of miles further west, in a deep tree-clad ravine, are the **Falls of Cruachan.**

We are now in the **Pass of Brander**—some 3 miles in length— enclosing a narrow tapering arm of Loch Awe. The east side is bounded by the steeps which form the base of Cruachan. In places the crags rise almost perpendicularly from the water and are thickly overgrown with trees of various kinds. Along the west side of the Pass lies a wall of sheer and barren crags. Behind, they rise in rough, uneven and heavy acclivities, but in front they terminate in precipices which form the whole side of the Pass. At the north end of the barrier "the arm of the loch gradually contracts its water to a very narrow space, and at length terminates at two rocks (called the Rocks of Brander) which form a straight channel, something resembling the lock of a canal. From this outlet there is a continual descent towards Loch Etive, the river pouring its current in a furious stream, foaming over a bed broken with holes and cumbered with masses of granite and other rocks."

The **Pass of Awe** begins where the loch arm ends and the river rushes out. A barrage here forms part of the Loch Awe Hydro-Electric Scheme (*see* p. 53). This was the scene of many a fierce fight between the MacNaughtons, the MacGregors, and other rival clans, numerous burial cairns marking the spots. Robert the Bruce and Sir James Douglas forced their way through the Pass ("ane evill place," according to Barbour's *The Brus*) in 1308, after laying low their Lorne opponents, and went on to besiege Dunstaffnage.

Spanning the stream, about 7 miles from Loch Awe pier, is the **Bridge of Awe.** Crossing the river, we emerge from the

shadow of Cruachan. On the north is the mansion-house of
Inverawe, whence Argyll set out to plunder "the bonnie house o'
Airlie," and where, about 1756, Major Duncan Campbell had
the tragic Ticonderoga Vision, which forms the subject of one
of Sir Thomas Dick Lauder's *Tales of the Highlands.* Almost
immediately we arrive at **Taynuilt** (*hotel*: angling), 9½ miles from
Loch Awe pier and about 12½ miles from Oban. It commands
a panorama of a large portion of Loch Etive, with the "braes
abune Bonawe," overtopped by Beinn Duirinnis (1,821 feet), on
the north, and Glen Salach lying ahead on the north-west.

Taynuilt is at the northern end of **Glen Nant.** Charming in
itself, the region is also much visited as an approach to Loch
Awe at Kilchrenan (*see* p. 59). It was a busy iron-smelting centre
in the days of charcoal furnaces (*see* p. 76). A granite monolith
commemorates Trafalgar and indicates the chief industry of
later times, quarrying.

Taynuilt is connected with Oban by bus as well as rail. It is a starting
point for the ascent of Cruachan (*see* p. 60). For walkers, besides the Pass
of Brander, Glen Nant, and Loch Etive side, there is an attractive route
through Glen Lonan to Loch Nell and Oban (*see* p. 40).

On the shore of the loch, about a mile from Taynuilt station,
is the village of **Bonawe,** opposite extensive granite quarries.

As we proceed, the upper bend of **Loch Etive,** stretching away
among the hills, breaks in upon the view on the north-east. In
summer one can sail up this enchanting loch from Ach-na-Cloich
—midway between Taynuilt and Connel—to **Lochetivehead, a**
lonely spot guarded by mighty Ben Starav (3,541 feet) and girdled
with lofty heights (*see* p. 76). There is no road along either side
of Loch Etive east of Bonawe.

The way westward to Connel (7 miles from Taynuilt) passes
through the State Forest of Fearnoch. The former railway
bridge at **Connel** (*see* p. 42) across Loch Etive has been reconstructed to take cars and walkers, thus opening up the route
to Ballachulish described on pp. 43-5

From Connel our road continues to skirt the shore, with
grand views across the water; it bears inland at Dunstaffnage
Bay (*see* p. 40) and **Oban** (22 miles from Loch Awe pier by road

or 25 by rail from Dalmally) suddenly reveals itself below, with the beautiful Kerrera Sound and island beyond.

To Loch Awe by Glen Nant.—Glen Nant, which mounts southwards from Taynuilt, is a popular route to Loch Awe from Oban. The main road (A85) to Taynuilt (12½ miles) has already been described (*see* p. 40). Taynuilt can also be reached from Oban by an upland secondary road *via* Glencruitten and Glen Lonan.

Crossing the bridge east of Taynuilt, we proceed up the right bank of the river *Nant* (by B845) through pleasant woods to a charming spot (2 miles from Taynuilt) known as the **Tailor's Leap,** from the tradition that a tailor, a notorious illicit distiller, here leaped across when pursued by excisemen. Rustic bridges lead to a picturesque fall, 40 feet in height, down which a tributary throws itself into the Nant. About a mile further on, the Nant turns south-westwards for Loch Nant, (now converted to reservoir). The road reaches its highest point (515 feet) on Barachander Hill, nearly 5 miles from Taynuilt. To the north, tower the twin peaks of Cruachan. Ben Lui may be seen in the east, Ben Buie and Ben Ime rather more to the south. We now drop down past Loch Tromlee to **Kilchrenan** ("the church on the little craig"). The old graveyard of Kilchrenan contains a massive granite monument erected by a Duke of Argyll in memory of his ancestor, Cailean Mor ("Great Colin"), to whom the Campbells owe the foundation of their greatness. He was the hero of many of the clan's forays and it was while returning from one of these in 1294 that he was slain by an arrow shot by an enemy lying in ambush on the Streng of Lorne, north of Loch Avich, where a large cairn marks the exact spot.

At **Taychreggan** (good angling) the road ends at the side of Loch Awe, opposite Portsonachan, on the eastern bank. Taychreggan (8 miles from Taynuilt, 20 from Oban) is beautifully situated and the sound of cowbells on the Highland cattle across the loch often adds to its romantic charm.

A good road runs up the loch to Inverinan—the Lodge is now an hotel —and on through the Forest to the *Avich*, about 7 miles from Kilchrenan. Turning up that impetuous little river, it comes in a mile and a half to **Loch Avich,** Ossian's Loch Launa, a picturesque sheet, over 3 miles long and perched 200 feet above the level of Loch Awe, amid scenes of Highland grandeur. The road takes the north side of the loch, from which a track leads up for a couple of miles, past Loch na Sreinge, to the cairn where Cailean Mor fell (*see* p. 59). From Loch Avich the road continues westward to join the Oban-Ardrishaig road at Kilmelfort (18 miles from Taychreggan, *see* p. 47).

IV.—CRUACHAN

The massive Cruachan Range has two crests. The eastern (or Dalmally) peak, properly *Cruachan Beann*, has an elevation of 3,689 feet, and the western (or Taynuilt) peak, *Stob Dearg*, is 3,611 feet high. They are three-quarters of a mile apart. The connecting ridge is some 3,400 feet in height.

The western peak commands the better view, as from it there is in sight more of the low ground near at hand than can be seen from the loftier summit. It also has the recommendation of affording the easier ascent from Oban. Visitors there should take a train or a bus to **Taynuilt** or motor to the Bridge of Awe (p. 57), a mile or so east of Taynuilt on the Dalmally road. On the far side of the bridge a road runs back on the east side of the river, and just beyond the railway line a path loops northward and then eastward and crosses the Allt Cruiniche high up near its source. Another track leaves the main road where it crosses the Allt Cruiniche, half a mile beyond Bridge of Awe. At first the course of the Allt Cruiniche must be followed, but at a respectful distance on account of the precipitous sides of its channel. Certain large and conspicuous boulders also serve to indicate a great portion of the route. The first is at a height of about 370 feet. The next is at a height of some 1,200 feet, is rectangular in shape, and has a perfectly flat top. About 300 feet higher is the confluence of the chief streams forming the Cruiniche. The route runs alongside the branch that comes down from the right, and a straight course should be steered for the neck of Cruachan. There lies a gigantic boulder, capped by stones that climbers have pitched upon it. It is at a height of 3,000 feet. Below is vegetation; above are bare granite rocks, and over them the way is far more toilsome than on the lower portion of the mountain. Care should be taken when the summit is reached not to approach too closely to the north side, especially if a strong wind is blowing, as there are dangerous precipices.

From its position, no less than its altitude, Cruachan presents some of the finest and most extensive mountain views in Scotland. From the bold granite precipices of its sharp and rugged summit, which is pointed, we look down upon its red and furrowed sides into the upper part of Loch Etive, and over the magnificent group of mountains which, extending north and east, form one of the finest landscapes in the Highlands.

The view during the ascent includes—

1. Westward—The lower portion of Loch Etive, Dunstaffnage, and the mountains of Mull and Morvern.

2. Southward—A great portion of Loch Awe.

3. Towards the south-west—Lochs Nell and Feochan and the Paps of Jura.

From the summit of the Taynuilt peak one may see—

1. Eastward—The Dalmally peak, Ben Lui, Ben Buie, Ben Ime and Ben Lomond.

2. Towards the north-east—The upper portion of Loch Etive, the Glencoe heights and Ben Nevis.

3. Southward—Loch Fyne and the heights in the Isle of Arran.

From the Dalmally peak there are added to the view eastward the twin peaks of Ben More and Stobinian in Perthshire, Ben Lawers (more distant and a point or two to the north), and Schiehallion (still farther away, and still more to the north).

The path for the **Falls of Cruachan** off the main road (6 miles from Taynuilt) is a good starting-point for the ascent of the eastern peak. The route lies up the western side of the *Allt Cruachan* and then a branch of the stream shows the way to a ridge on the left connecting a prominent shoulder (*Meall Cuanail*, 3,004 feet) with the main peak. When the ridge (2,750 feet) is scaled the route lies to the right.

The descent from the summit will be made most easily along the line of the ascent, but those who desire to vary the route and do not fear a longer tramp, may "do" the two summits and combine the two routes described; while hardy mountaineers may strike eastwards from the summit along the main ridge by *Drochaid Glas* (3,312 feet) and *Stob Diamh* (3,272 feet), and descend by the "Horseshoe" to the main road at the mouth of

Glen Strae, between Loch Awe pier (1½ miles) and Dalmally (3 miles). The complete traverse of the main ridge of Cruachan is a very fine expedition for experienced climbers *in clear weather*.

Underground Power Station.—An access road to the new dam on Ben Cruachan leaves the main road (A85) three-quarters of a mile west of Loch Awe Hotel. The road is open to walkers but because the hillside is so steep great care must be taken not to dislodge stones which might cause interference to the Dalmally-Oban railway line ot to the A85. The road is only open to vehicular traffic by prior permission of the Hydro-Electric Board. The underground power station is open to the public but here too permission must first be obtained.

V.—TO KILLIN AND LOCH TAY

By train to Crianlarich, thence bus to Killin.

By road, which closely follows the track of the railway, Oban is 56 miles from Killin; Killin to Kenmore by the north side of Loch Tay, 16¼ miles; Kenmore to Killin by the south side (poorer surface, sharper hills, but finer views than on the main road (A827) on the northern bank), 17 miles.

Along the route are Dunstaffnage Castle, Loch Etive, Pass of Brander, Cruachan, Loch Awe, Kilchurn Castle, Glen Orchy, Ben More, Glen Dochart, Killin, Loch Tay, and Ben Lawers. Most of these have already been noticed.

The pretty village of **Killin** (Kill*in*) is said to derive its name from *Keil* and *Fin*, signifying the grave of Fin or Fingal, the great hero of Gaelic mythology, and a granite rock is pointed out as marking his last resting-place.

The village is considered one of the most picturesque in Scotland. It is situated amid mountains, at the junction of the *Lochay* and the *Dochart*, the head waters of the Tay. Killin has a 9-hole golf course, a Youth Hostel and excellent hotels, and is an angling, mountaineering, and ski-ing centre.

Killin is situated at the head of—

Loch Tay

one of the largest and most beautiful lochs of Scotland. About 15 miles long and a mile broad, Loch Tay is fringed on both sides by high hills. For salmon-fishing it has long been famed.

Salmon fishing begins on January 15, and may be enjoyed by visitors at the following hotels: *Killin, Morenish, Ben Lawers* (Lawers), *Tigh-an-loan* (Fearnan), and *Kenmore* (Kenmore).

Trout fishing can be arranged through these hotels. Permits for fishing tributary rivers from newsagent shop in Killin.

The steamer service, which used to be in operation in the summer months, has unfortunately not been resumed since the War, but a motor service by the north side connects Killin with Fearnan, near the other end of the Loch, Fortingall, and Aberfeldy.

At the head of the Loch, eastward of Killin, **Kinnell House,** home of the present chief of Clan Macnab, has a vine famed for its size and age. Near by is a large hydro-electric station. On an island (Innis Bhuidhe) below the Dochart Bridge is the picturesque old burying-ground of the Macnabs, whose country was in Glen Dochart before they emigrated to Canada. Between the village and the pier are the ivy-clad ruins of **Finlarig Castle,** one of the earliest seats of the Breadalbane family.

North of the loch, some 2 miles from Killin, a branch road leads off to Glen Lochay, about 8 miles long.

Some 4 miles along the north side of Loch Tay, a hill road strikes off boldly for Bridge of Balgie in Glen Lyon, climbing abruptly to over 1,600 feet. Lochan Na Lairige, near the top, feeds a generating station on Loch Tay under the Lawers Hydro-Electric scheme. About mid-way down the Loch, Lawers (*hotel*) nestles at the foot of towering **Ben Lawers** (3,984 feet), which ranks ninth among the mountains of Scotland. Nevertheless, it is of comparatively gentle ascent. A favourite ski-ing ground, Ben Lawers is now mainly National Trust property. It is noted for its rare alpine plants.

From **Fearnan** (*Tigh-an-loan*), a picturesque village 3 miles from the eastern end of Loch Tay, a road runs due north to Fortingall, in **Glen Lyon,** a narrow glen about 30 miles long—the longest in Scotland—with magnificent scenery and much legendary lore. **Fortingall** has a venerable yew-tree, an excellent hotel, and a Youth Hostel (Garth) with a Field Studies Centre. A mail van runs up Glen Lyon to Bridge of Balgie.

Really good walkers can be recommended to explore the Glen to Loch Lyon (there is a huge new dam at Lynn Lyon) at its head, whence a path leads over (below Ben Douran) to the Glencoe Road, midway between Bridge of Orchy and Tyndrum; or to take the moorland track northward from Innerwick to Dall, on Loch Rannoch, 6 miles west of Kinloch-Rannoch (*hotels*) and 12 miles east of Rannoch station (West Highland Line).

Beyond Fearnan is the wood-covered and deer-frequented **Drummond Hill.** Near this end of the loch a small but pretty island contains the ruins of a priory, founded in 1122 by Alexander I, whose first queen, Sibylla, daughter of Henry I of England, was buried in it.

At **Kenmore,** an attractive village gathered round a green, the River Tay issues full-grown from the Loch. Beside the green are the church, the *Breadalbane Hotel*, and an entrance to *Taymouth Castle*, formerly a seat of the Marquis of Breadalbane, then in turn an hotel, a Polish Military hospital, and a Civil Defence Training School. There is a golf course in the grounds.

On the southern shore of Loch Tay, **Acharn,** 2 miles from Kenmore, has picturesque Falls (half a mile from the road).

VI.—TO THE TROSSACHS

Leave Oban by train for Crianlarich, thence by motor-coach to the Trossachs, returning the same way. (*See* current time-tables.) There are motor-coach tours from Oban to the Trossachs in the season.

By road it is 78 miles to Loch Katrine *via* Dalmally, Crianlarich, and Lochearnhead, traversing *en route* the Pass of Brander and Glens Lochy, Dochart, and Ogle. Between Dalmally and Tyndrum a height of 900 feet is reached, and between Luib and Lochearnhead 945 feet.

The road from Callander to the Trossachs ends at Loch Katrine, where there is a large car park, but on fine summer days congestion may occur at this *cul-de-sac*. The road over the hills from the Trossachs to Aberfoyle offers a very inviting—if longer—alternative return route to Oban *via* Drymen, Balloch, and Loch Lomond (*see* p. 67).

The road route to **Callander** has been described in the reverse direction on pp. 20-1.

Callander is a neat little town, well provided with hotels (*Dreadnought*, *Ancaster Arms*, *Caledonian*, etc.). Through it flows the river *Teith*, crossed by a bridge with a fine view of the **Pass of Leny,** a wild, narrow, rocky ravine, along which run the road and railway to Lochearnhead and Oban. A short walk over the shoulder of the hill at the back of the town leads to the **Bracklinn Falls,** on the Keltie Water.

Visitors can fish the Teith and neighbouring lochs, there is a golf course and numerous pleasant excursions can be taken from Callander (*see* our *Red Guide to the Highlands* and our *Complete Scotland*).

Dalmally, and Ben Cruachan (*Wm. S. Thomson*)

Loch Awe, near Portsonachan (*Wm. S. Thomson*)

Kilchurn Castle, Loch Awe (*J. Salmon Ltd.*)

Glencoe Village and Pap of Glencoe (*J. Salmon*)*Ltd.*

The first portion of the route from Callander to the Trossachs is interesting largely by reason of the glamour which has been thrown over it by Sir Walter Scott, for the road (A821) along which one travels to Loch Katrine follows the line of the chase described in *The Lady of the Lake*.

Immediately to the west of Callander is the farmhouse of **Bochastle,** standing on the left. The hunt, it will be remembered, passed over Bochastle Heath. Then, at the foot of Loch Vennachar, is the site of **Coilantogle Ford,** where Roderick Dhu defied FitzJames. In place of the ford there will be seen a bridge and the sluices that guard the exit from the loch to compensate by storage for the water drained off farther up to supply the city of Glasgow. From here a path leads to the top of **Ben Ledi** (2,873 feet), from which there is a magnificent view.

Loch Vennachar, "the Loch of the Fair Valley," is a lovely sheet of water, 4 miles in length. It holds trout, perch, and pike, "and a salmon is no very unusual capture." Ahead there comes into sight **Ben Venue** (2,393 feet), the sentinel on the left hand of the Trossachs Pass. Near the western extremity of the loch is **Lanrick Mead,** the muster place of the Clan Alpine, where the warriors of Roderick Dhu arose in answer to the chieftain's "whistle shrill."

Lendrick, formerly a shooting lodge, at the west end of Loch Vennachar, is now a Youth Hostel. Then—a favourite haunt of artists and of hikers—appears the famous **Brig o' Turk,** spanning the *Finglas*. The water in this glen is now impounded and led into Loch Katrine to increase the Glasgow supply. Beyond the bridge there lies enchanting **Loch Achray,** some 2 miles long, its shores wooded to the water's edge. The Forestry Commission area south of Loch Achray (*hotel*) forms part of the Queen Elizabeth National Forest Park.

Near the western extremity stand the church and manse of the **Trossachs** (the

"rough country"), one or two villas and the *Trossachs Hotel* (8¼ miles from Callander).

Here we enter the famous pass of—

The Trossachs

a romantic wooded gorge about a mile long. "There are glens in Scotland surrounded by loftier hills and presenting, on a greater scale, breadth, depth, and wild magnificence . . . but the rugged gorge of the Trossachs possesses excellencies peculiarly its own, unparalleled in the scenery of Scotland. Every turn of the road unfolds fresh views of wild and romantic beauty. The valley is one continuous maze of rugged mountains, grey rocks and green woods, lofty precipices and dark ravines, shimmering cliffs and heathery knolls with masses of trees dispersed in picturesque confusion."

The road that makes easy the tourist's passage through the Trossachs has robbed the gorge of some of its original wildness.

The pass suddenly opens out at the eastern end of **Loch Katrine,** a celebrated sheet of water hemmed in by Ben Venue and Ben A'an (1,750 feet). The loch is about 8 miles in length and of varying width, the average being three-quarters of a mile, while the widest part is about 2 miles across. The Trossachs end is by far the most beautiful portion. Many islands, large and small, break its surface. The most interesting is **Ellen's Isle,** "bosky as when James FitzJames saw Ellen's skiff dart from its side." It is not far from the steamer pier. Ellen's Isle was one of the last fastnesses of the MacGregor clansmen.

Independently of its beauty, Loch Katrine is notable among the lochs of Scotland as the reservoir for the city of Glasgow 34 miles distant by the route along which the water is carried. The first aqueduct and works were opened by Queen Victoria in 1859. The raising of the level of Loch Katrine unhappily involved the submerging of the "Silver Strand."

The main road ends at the steamer pier, but a private road continues for 5 or 6 miles along the northern side of the Loch to Strone, and a path continues this road up Strath Gartney to **Glen Gyle** ($8\frac{1}{2}$ miles) at the head of the Loch, Rob Roy's birthplace (1671), whence another path leads round a few miles to **Stronachlachar** (*see* p. 68).

Motorists were long compelled to return from the Trossachs to Callander by the way they came; but the rebuilt "Duke's Road" (till 1932 a toll road closed to motor traffic) climbs over to Aberfoyle (6 miles to the south) from the head of Loch Achray. It zigzags west of Loch Drunkie through the Queen Elizabeth Forest Park and provides an alternative return to Callander, as well as a handy route to Glasgow and to Loch Lomond. The "clachan" of Aberfoyle, immortalized in Scott's *Rob Roy*, is today a popular holiday resort, with angling, a 9-hole golf course and a choice of hotels (*Bailie Nicol Jarvie* is the best known).

VII.—LOCH LOMOND *via* THE TROSSACHS

In summer, on weekdays—in connection with a popular circular tour—a steamer sails along Loch Katrine between Trossachs Pier and Sronachlachar, which is linked by motor-coach with Inversnaid on Loch Lomond.

Motorists.—The Loch steamers do not carry cars. If motorists use the Achray-Aberfoyle road and go thence by Drymen to Balloch, at the south end of Loch Lomond, they may return towards Oban by the lovely road along the western banks of Loch Lomond. From Ardlui, at the north end of the loch, the route is *via* Crianlarich and Tyndrum as described on pp. 20-1.

Hikers are well provided for in this world-famous region. There are excellent S.Y.H.A. hostels at the west end of Loch Vennachar, near Brig o'Turk; at the west end of Loch Ard, 4 miles from Aberfoyle; at Rowardennan on the east side of Loch Lomond, at the foot of Ben Lomond; and on the west bank at Arden (near the south end of the Loch) and Inverbeg (opposite Rowardennan: ferry). The **Queen Elizabeth National Forest Park** (*see* p. 11) extends between the Trossachs and Loch Lomond, and this Rob Roy country is now being developed and improved for public use.

This excursion is identical with that just described as far as Loch Katrine—the Cateran (freebooter) Loch.

Here the little steamer receives its passengers at a rustic pier, and it soon carries them past **Ellen's Isle** (*see* p. 66). Then as the vessel advances the scenery grows tamer and shows the effects of man's utilitarian schemes. The western end of the loch leads away to **Glen Gyle,** the home of the MacGregors, the birthplace of Rob Roy. The voyage ends at **Stronachlachar** ("the Stone-mason's Point"), about 2 miles from the head of the loch.

The next section of the route (5 miles in length) is by road (the famous old horse coach was superseded by motor-coach in 1938), passing little **Loch Arklet,** the level of which has been consider-ably raised to increase Glasgow's water supply. (From the east end of Loch Arklet a road runs southwards to Aberfoyle, $11\frac{1}{2}$ miles from Stronachlachar, by the lovely waters of Loch Chon and Loch Ard, which gives its name to part of the Queen Eliza-beth Forest Park.) Four miles from Stronachlachar the road passes "the Garrison," the site of a fort built in 1713 to overawe the clansmen, but it was surprised and dismantled both by Rob Roy and his nephew. It is said to have been commanded at one time by Wolfe, the hero of Quebec. The end of the drive is at Rob Roy's fastness of **Inversnaid** (*hotel*), reached by a very steep zigzag. Here it was that Sir Walter Scott pictured Rob Roy bidding farewell to Bailie Nicol Jarvie. The cave that can be seen in the face of the rock a mile up Lomondside is said to have sheltered not only Rob Roy but King Robert the Bruce. At Inversnaid, too, Wordsworth saw the Highland girl, the handmaid of the rustic hostelry of that day, who inspired him to sing the charms of—

> "The cabin small,
> The lake, the bay, the waterfall."

The waterfall is on the Arklet, which flows into the loch at Inversnaid. There is no road from Inversnaid either up or down Loch Lomond, but paths lead north to Ardlui and south to Rowardennan, and there is a ferry (passengers and cycles only) to Inveruglas, across the Loch (*see* p. 21).

Loch Lomond

During the season there are coach tours from Oban to Loch Lomond. In summer (June to mid-September) a steamer sails daily from end to end of the loch, from Balloch to Ardlui and back, calling at Balmaha, Rowar-dennan, Tarbet, and Inversnaid—an entertaining trip.

Loch Lomond is about 23 miles in length, and its greatest width is 5 miles. For beauty it is justly famed, and it is in high repute among anglers. In area, nearly 27½ sq. miles, Loch Lomond is the largest lake in Britain, the deepest part, some 600 feet, being a mile south of Inversnaid. Barely a quarter of the lovely lake is traversed in passing by steamer from Inversnaid to Ardlui at its head. Close to Ardlui Pier is a station on the West Highland line.

The Loch is fully described in our *Red Guide to the Highlands.*

From Ardlui the route (by train or road) lies up "green Glenfalloch," 8 miles long, and at the end is **Crianlarich,** whence the route to Oban is as described on p. 20.

VIII.—TO GLENCOE

Motorists.—The best road route is by Connel and Dalmally to Clifton, just short of Tyndrum, where is the beginning of the fine road by Bridge of Orchy to Glencoe and Ballachulish (*see* p. 26).

The alternative, which can be used to make a circular tour of *c.* 100 miles (it is better, for scenic reasons, to *return* by the Glencoe road), is *via* Connel Bridge (*see* p. 42) and thence by the winding road through Appin and along the shore of Loch Linnhe to Ballachulish.

A delightful circular trip is available on certain days, viz. motor-coach by Tyndrum, Glencoe, and Loch Leven to Fort William, and return thence to Oban by MacBrayne steamer.

In the holiday months there are frequent excursions to Glencoe from Oban by motor-coach.

By Ballachulish.—The Ballachulish road (A828) as far as Barcaldine has already been described (*see* pp. 43-5). After crossing the peninsula of Benderloch and passing the ancient keep of **Barcaldine,** the road follows the lovely **Loch Creran,** a long, winding arm of the sea, on whose low islets white sea-swallows make their nests and seals often bask. The end of the loch and the small river Creran is crossed by Creran Bridge before the road turns along the northern shore of the loch to North Creran. About a mile farther on is **Invernahyle,** the seat of Donald of the Hammer, who led the Stewarts of Appin at the battle of Pinkie in 1547. In his "teens" Sir Walter Scott used to visit his father's client, Alexander Stewart of Invernahyle.

Northward of Loch Creran, on an islet opposite Appin, stands the square ruined tower of **Castle Stalker**, built by Duncan Stewart of Appin as a hunting lodge in which to entertain his royal relative, James IV. In those days the Stewarts of Appin, "the gallant, devoted old Stewarts of Appin," as the Ettrick Shepherd calls them in his ballad, held the whole region of Appin—"**Green Appin**" extending from Loch Creran to Ballachulish. A couple of miles west of Appin Church is Port Appin (*Aird's*), facing the northern tip of Lismore Island; about the same distance north, Appin House looks out on the island of

Shuna

For the part the Stewarts of Appin took in the rebellion of 1745 their estates were forfeited, and the management of these was entrusted by the Government to Colin Campbell of Glenure (in the same district), whose assassination (May 14, 1752) forms the notorious event known as the **Appin Murder,** familiar to readers of R. L. Stevenson's *Kidnapped* and *Catriona*.

Alan Breck, one of Stevenson's characters, was suspected, but he managed to escape to France; and James Stewart ("James of the Glens"), the illegitimate half-brother of Stewart of Appin, who had been heard to utter words that were construed as a threat against the factor, was arrested, tried, found guilty by a Campbell jury, as an accessory, and hanged on a little mound (with a memorial) close to Ballachulish Ferry. Another monument, north of Duror Hotel and church, marks the scene of the murder.

The road now goes inland at Duror, to cross the promontory of Ardsheal, comes out on the shore again at Kentallen and winds round the skirts of Ben Vair or Sgorr Dhonuill (3,284 feet), and of Creag Ghorm (2,372 feet), and the wood of Lettermore to Ballachulish Ferry, at the entrance to Loch Leven.

Ballachulish (*Ballachulish, Laroch;* 39 miles by road from Oban, is a slate-built village situated on the south side of **Loch Leven**). It was formerly busy with the export of roofing slates, some of the largest slate quarries in Scotland, now unused, being in the neighbourhood. The village stands in the midst of magnificent scenery, and offers facilities for boating and sea-fishing. For the **Ferry**, *see* p. 95.

From Ballachulish the road runs eastward to the little clachan of Carnach (*Glencoe Hotel*) beyond which it begins to ascend—

Glencoe

which maintains its air of wild grandeur notwithstanding the broad modern highway and the constant stream of cars. (Walkers will find a more attractive way along the *old* road *via* Bridge of Coe, the Youth Hostel, and Clachaig.)

Glencoe is among the grandest and most magnificent glens in Scotland. Macaulay's description in his *History of England* will be familiar to many.

"In the Gaelic tongue," he tells us, "Glencoe signifies the Glen of Weeping; and in truth, that pass is the most dreary and melancholy of all the Scottish passes—the very Valley of the Shadow of Death. Mists and storms brood over it through the greater part of the finest summer; and even on those rare days when the sun is bright, and when there is no cloud in the sky, the impression made by the landscape is sad and awful."

Now, to begin with, Glencoe does *not* mean the Glen of Weeping in Gaelic. Sunny days are by no means rare and while the Glen has a

brooding atmosphere of its own, the impression it makes on the average visitor is far from that of horror such as Macaulay and Dickens, among others, ascribe to it.

A more accurate description of the Glen is conveyed by Andrew Lang—

"I write in Glencoe, one of the most beautiful valleys in the beautiful West Highlands. Macaulay gave the place a bad name; I presume he saw it on a wet day, or thought it a less crime in a Whig to massacre people who lived in a desolate spot. The Coe is as clear as the Itchen; the loch lies a sheet of silver washed with gold; the inhabitants are an industrious populace, great as volunteers, full of old traditions, and not too incredulous about the second sight. . . .

"Up the glen did Alan Breck and David Balfour escape after the Appin murder. But you will look in vain for the big stone on the top of which they 'birstled' or toasted in the sun. As to their famous leap over the linn, it was quite needless; they could easily have forded the burn at a hundred places. Otherwise the scene is very like the description in *Kidnapped*, the big, steep, weatherworn stumps of hills frowning all around."

The Massacre of Glencoe.—At the time of the event, this part of the country belonged to a branch of the clan Macdonald. William III had been seated on the throne from which James II had fled, but the change of sovereigns was not pleasing to all British subjects, and among the discontented were the Highlanders.

In 1691 the clans were required to take, before the end of the year, the oath of allegiance to William III. All submitted except the clansmen of Glencoe. Their chief, MacIan, an old man, held out to the last day. Then, realizing the folly of resistance, he hastened to Fort William to take the oath, but there was no magistrate in the garrison to receive him. The nearest was at Inveraray, and thither MacIan hurried, but the mountain passes were deep with snow, and it was not until January 6 that he achieved his purpose.

The magistrates administered the oath, and duly notified the fact to the authorities at Edinburgh. But by their raids the Macdonalds had made many enemies, who now seized the opportunity to have vengeance. The magistrate's explanation of MacIan's delay was withheld from the King's advisers, who were persuaded to cancel the certificate of submission by what were known as Letters of Fire and Sword, and obtain the royal warrant for the extirpation of the clan.

The punitive force consisted of a hundred and twenty men, commanded by Captain Campbell of Glenlyon. The original order under which this hereditary enemy of the Macdonalds acted may be seen in the National Library of Scotland in Edinburgh. The soldiers entered the glen under a plausible pretext, and the old chief, suspecting no evil, treated them with Highland hospitality. For twelve days they were entertained by the Macdonalds, and on the very night of the fell deed the commander was playing cards with the chieftain's son.

At five o'clock on the morning of February 13, 1692, the massacre began. By dawn well-nigh two score corpses strewed the ground—among them at least one woman, an old man of seventy and a child o four. Some 150 men and a like number of women fled, but a great number of the fugitives perished among the snowy heights. The old chief was shot as he got out of bed.

When the butchery was over the deserted huts were fired, and the executioners departed, driving before them the flocks and herds and Highland ponies that had belonged to the clan.

The whole upper part of Glencoe is (since 1937) the property of the National Trust for Scotland, the boundaries being—the north ridge of Glencoe (*Aonach Eagach*: 3,168 feet) from above Clachaig to Am Bodach, then over beside the road to Altnafeadh, down the river Coupal to its junction with the river Etive and along the latter to Dalness, thence north-west by the ridge of Bidean nam Bian to Clachaig. The total area thus ensured against undesirable exploitation is about 12,000 acres. The surrounding mountains provide the finest rock climbing in Scotland.

The new road, like the old, strikes off from the Loch side at Carnach (*Glencoe Hotel*), a mile or so to the east of Ballachulish. The old road, however, quickly crosses the Coe by Bridge of Coe and passes a monument commemorating the Massacre. Nearby is Glencoe House, now a hospital, but once the mansion of Lord Strathcona, of Hudson's Bay Company and Canadian Pacific Railway fame. About a mile from Carnach is a much-frequented Youth Hostel (of Norwegian timber). A mile or two up the glen on the same side clusters of green mounds and grey stones mark the sites of the ruined huts of the clan. At the head of the wider part of the glen rises the **Signal Rock,** which owes its name to the tradition that it was the spot whence was given the signal for the massacre. (A foot-bridge connects it with the main road.) Close above this spot stands the *Clachaig Inn*, 6 miles from Ballachulish Ferry.

Beyond Clachaig the two roads join, the new road having thus far kept to the left bank. In front rises the precipice of the **Black Rock** of Glencoe, with the lonely tarn, **Loch Achtriochtan,** at its foot. High in the face of the Black Rock is a narrow but deep recess known as **Ossian's Cave,** and **Ossian's Shower Bath** may be seen in a corrie close by. Ossian is said to have been born beside Loch Achtriochtan. At the head of the pass, high above the river gorge through which the road now goes, is a terrace known as the **Study** (a Scots word for the Anvil). From it the best view of the glen can be obtained. Looking down the glen from this point, one sees on the left three remarkable mountain masses commonly called the **"Three Sisters of Glencoe."**

Beyond the summit of the pass, a track on the left, known as the **Devil's Staircase,** climbs over to the head of Loch Leven. This was an old military road (*c.* 1750). The path was the route taken by the two young sons of the chief of the Macdonalds in escaping from the massacre of their clan.

Beyond this the glen opens out and the road, after crossing the watershed (1,024 feet), crosses the River Etive and passes a quarter of a mile to the west of *Kingshouse Hotel*, which is on the old road on the other side of the river. The road now runs south-east on to **Rannoch Moor** (declared a National Nature Reserve in 1958), rounds the north-east shoulder of Beinn Chaorach at a height of 1,143 feet (the highest point on the new road) and descends to the west end of Loch Ba. Passing between that loch and Lochan na h-Achlaise, the road strikes southward and drops rapidly down to the east end of Loch Tulla, and thence along the south side of that loch to **Bridge of Orchy.** (*Inveroran Hotel* is 2½ miles distant on the old road at the west end of the loch.) From Bridge of Orchy (whence a secondary road runs down Glen Orchy to Dalmally) the new road keeps to the west side of the glen containing the railway and, after crossing into Perthshire at a height of 1,033 feet, reaches the Oban road at Clifton, half a mile west from **Tyndrum** (*hotel*). Clifton is named after the English contractor of lead mines worked here from 1741.

Glen Etive.—At the head of Glen Etive, **Kingshouse** owes its name to its having served as quarters for troops engaged in making military roads in the eighteenth century. Today it is a popular climbing centre for the Glencoe peaks and crags. On Meall a Bhuiridh (the "Hill of the Roaring Stags": 3,636 feet), a couple of miles south of Kingshouse, the Scottish Ski Club built the first ski-tow in Britain (1955).

A mile west of Kingshouse, a side-road strikes south-west, between **Buachaille Etive Mor,** the "Big Herdsman of Etive" (3,345 feet) and the **Clachlet** (*Clach Leathad:* 3,602 feet), and makes its way down Glen Etive. In front, on the left, rises Ben Ceitlin, with Grianan Deirdeuil, "Deirdre's sunning-place," on its slope and a fine waterfall at its foot. Glen Etive, according to legend, was the happy retreat of Deirdre when she fled from Ireland.

In the angle formed by Glencoe and Glen Etive is the ancient deer forest of **Dalness,** which forms the western and southern portion of the National Trust property.

Near Dalness, a footpath, not well-marked, leads off northward between *Beinn Fhada* (3,497 feet), one of the "Three Sisters of Glencoe," and *Buachaille Etive Beag* (the "Little Herdsman," 3,130 feet) to Glencoe. It is rough walking (4 miles) in lonely country.

From Dalness the road runs down the widening strath, till ahead there appear the waters of **Loch Etive** shining between the hills. The road ends at the head of the loch, which is an inlet of the sea about 20 miles in length and of varying width. At the broadest part it is only a mile and a half across. Lochetivehead is 13 miles from Kingshouse, 27 miles from Ballachulish Ferry, and (by water—there is no road, and only a rough path, on either side) 11 miles from Bonawe, 14 from Ach-na-Cloich, which is 9½ miles by rail from Oban.

On the north side of the Loch, where it is narrowest, half-way between its head and its mouth, are the great granite quarries of **Bonawe** (*see* p. 58), while on the south are the fine woods of **Inverawe House** and the village of Bonawe, which was formerly the scene of extensive operations for converting the woods of the district into charcoal and using it in the manufacture of pig iron, the ore being imported from Lancashire. Some 600 men were employed at the work. The furnaces were closed in 1863. The woody hillside behind the village is celebrated in the well-known song, *The Braes abune Bonawe.*

Looking up the loch from Bonawe, on the right one sees lofty **Cruachan** (p. 60). Far ahead rise the twin mountains **Buachaille Etive Mor** and **Beag.** On the east shore of the loch, at its head, is **Ben Starav** (3,541 feet), while **Ben Trilleachan** (2,752 feet) is on the west.

Almost opposite the rustic pier of **Ach-na-Cloich** is **Ardchattan Priory** (p. 45).

Excursions by Sea

1.—TO THE ISLAND OF MULL

Car ferry operates between Oban and Craignure, with bus or coach connection with Salen and Tobermory. On certain days there is a direct steamer Oban—Tobermory.

Mull is the third largest island of the Hebrides. In shape it is extremely irregular, and its coastline is so much indented that it measures quite 250 miles in circumference, while the longest walk in a bee line across the island would be but 30 miles, and the shortest barely 3. The area of Mull is 347 square miles; the present population, 2,000 to 3,000, is but a third of what it was a century ago.

The southern and eastern part is mountainous, the peaks varying from 1,500 to over 3,000 feet in height. The northern portion of the island is hilly, but no eminence attains an elevation of 1,500 feet.

The greatest indentation of the island is **Loch na Keal** (p. 83), on the western side. It is a favourite resort of seals, and at its head is a beautiful sandy beach. Coal is found at Ardtun, on the shore of the Loch, and the leaf-beds here are rich in fossils. The columnar shores and promontories of Loch na Keal and the Sound of Ulva are clothed with ivy and with oak and ash copses. The coast of Loch na Keal and the long promontory called the Ross of Mull are particularly interesting to geologists.

There is a ferry to Iona from Fionphort on the Ross. Daily motor tours are run to Iona and other places of interest. Though much of Mull can be seen in the course of a day's excursion from Oban, the island deserves more time, if only for its legendary lore.

A description of the northern shore will be found on pp. 82-3, of the western on p. 84, and of the southern on p. 91.

The island abounds in lochs, most of which contain yellow trout. The rivers also provide sport for anglers. The residents at some of the hotels have the right of fishing in certain waters.

The best point for those wishing to climb Ben More is **Salen** (MacBrayne's Craignure-Tobermory service), which commends itself to visitors by its central situation. There are churches, an hotel, and a post and telegraph office (known as **Aros,** to avoid confusion with Salen on Loch Sunart). The village is connected through Glen Aros with **Loch Frisa,** the largest freshwater loch in Mull (with boats for anglers). An easy road runs from Salen south-eastward to **Glen Forsa** (*Glen Forsa Guest House*), some 3 miles distant. In the woods of the glen and in the corries of the adjacent hills are many red deer.

Ascent of Ben More.—Ben More (3,169 feet) is the highest summit in the island. The ascent can be made with comparative ease. The distance from Salen to the foot of the Ben is 7 miles, and reckoning from that spot, the ascent and descent may be accomplished in from 3½ to 4½ hours.

The ascent can best be started from near Dishig, on the south shore of **Loch na Keal,** some 7 miles from Salen by the road (A849) which cuts across the low narrow neck of land separating the Sound of Mull from Loch na Keal and passes (3½ miles) over the river Ba not far from where it issues from **Loch Ba.** Almost opposite the island of Eorsa, leave the road and make for An Gearna, the north-east shoulder of the mountain, from which the ascent to the summit is simple, and no further directions are necessary.

By continuing on the same road one may reach **Mackinnon's Cave,** on the west coast, near Gribun (11½ miles from Salen). Legend has it that this cavern extends right across the island and that Mackinnon's piper, who ventured in to explore it, never returned to tell of his encounter with the Wee Folk, its fairy denizens. The cave, which can be entered only at low water, is reputed to be 100 yards long and 50 to 80 feet high. Dr. Johnson (who did not visit Staffa) declared it "the greatest natural curiosity" he had ever seen. The road goes southward from the mouth of Loch na Keal over to **Loch Scridain,** an even longer inlet of the sea, which it rounds. Joined by the Glen More road from Craignure, it then makes westward along the southern shore of Loch Scridain (*see* p. 86) for Bunessan (*Argyll Arms*) and Fionphort, where is the ferry for Iona. Fionphort is 39 miles from

Salen by this winding route and 36 miles from Craignure by the old pilgrim's way.

In the cliff-girt headlands of Armeanach, north of Loch Scridain, is *The Burg*, a 2,000-acre farm belonging to the National Trust for Scotland, where successful experiments were conducted in the reclamation of derelict land overrun with bracken. A sanctuary of wild life, it contains a famous fossil, **MacCulloch's Tree,** a great conifer embedded upright in rock.

From Salen to Tobermory by land is 10 miles. The road, a pleasant one, lies along the Sound of Mull and passes the ruin of **Aros Castle** (2½ miles from Salen), an ancient stronghold of the Lords of the Isles.

Tobermory

Early Closing.—Wednesdays.

Fishing.—Good deep-sea fishing available.

Hotels.—*Western Isles, Mishnish, MacDonald Arms:* also Guest Houses.

Population.—About 700.

Recreation.—Fishing, boating, bathing, tennis, and golf.

Steamers.—Car ferry Oban to Craignure thence road services. Direct steamer from Oban on certain days. To and from Mingary (in Ardnamurchan) daily, except Sunday (*see* p. 83).

Tobermory, "the Well of Mary," is the chief town in the Island of Mull. Founded in 1788 by the Society for the Encouragement of the British Fisheries, it has not realized the hopes of its founders by becoming an important fishing station. It stands on the shore of a bay which affords safe and spacious anchorage and is protected by the small island of Calve, much in the same way as Oban Bay is by Kerrera.

The chief street runs alongside the harbour, but there are many buildings—conspicuous among them the *Western Isles Hotel*—on the high ground at the back of this thoroughfare, and the whole as seen from the deck of an approaching steamer is exceedingly picturesque.

One of the ships of the Spanish Armada (some say the *Florida*, others the *Florencia*, others again the *San Juan Bautista*) was sunk in the Bay in 1588—according to local tradition, by Donald Glas MacLean, who, retained as a hostage, set fire to the magazine. In 1641-1642 the Marquess of Argyll obtained a royal gift of ships of the Armada sunk near Tobermory, with contents thought to be of great worth. Brass and iron guns, shot, silverplate, and other relics were recovered at various times, and in May 1950 Royal Navy divers located a very old hulk, deep in silt, and two silver medallions were brought up. The identity of the wreck and the presence of treasure aboard remain to be proved.

Dr. Johnson and Boswell paid a visit to Tobermory in October 1773. A storm, a tiring ride to Ulva, and the loss of his oak stick put Johnson out of humour with Mull.

Tobermory is a resort of summer visitors. It has an excellent water and electricity supply and its attractions include splendid scenery and excursions by steamer, motor-boat or motor-coach (to Iona, etc.), a 9-hole golf course, a cinema, Highland Games (in July), and a Regatta (August).

A small stream, which empties itself into the bay, tumbles over a pretty double cascade at the back of the town. Towards the north-west is **St. Mary's Well,** which gave its name to the place and was once believed to have healing virtues. The **Lighthouse** on Rudha nan Gall ("Stranger's Point"), on the cliffs at the northern extremity of the Bay, commands an extensive panorama. About 2 miles from the town are the Aros Waterfalls, in the beautiful grounds of **Aros House.** Five miles north-westward is **Glengorm Castle,** a modern building, with a magnificent sea view. A rather hilly road runs west by the Mishnish Lochs and Dervaig to the castle and sandy bay of **Calgary** (whose name was carried to Canada by Mull emigrants) and thence southward to Loch na Keal.

II.—TO STAFFA AND IONA

Steamer leaves about 9 a.m. and is due at Oban again about 6 p.m.

The boats for landing at Iona are large, each capable of carrying from forty to seventy passengers. The steamer passes close to Staffa to give passengers a good view of Fingal's Cave.

The voyage covers about 120 miles.

This excursion, the most popular sea trip from Oban, includes, except on Wednesdays, the circuit of Mull. In the season (June to mid-September) it takes place daily (except Sunday).

Proceeding across the Firth of Lorne towards the east shore of **Mull,** we pass the Dog Stone and Dunollie Castle, and go between Kerrera Island, on which the Hutcheson Obelisk is a conspicuous object, and the Maiden Island. Dunstaffnage Castle may be seen—by looking back—at the entrance to Loch Etive, and far east of that are the twin peaks of Cruachan.

Then the steamer makes for **Lismore Lighthouse.** "Lismore" is generally translated the "Great Garden," but in ancient Gaelic *lis* meant "a fort," not (as now) a "garden"; and it is argued that the island took its name, not from its fertile soil, but from the fortified monastery of Moluag, a Pictish saint, who, in the sixth century, established his chief cell here. In a coracle race for the island, says tradition, Moluag severed a finger and flung it ashore to forestall Columba. Before reaching Lismore (*see* p. 93) the summit of Ben Nevis may be described far up Loch Linnhe. Nearly opposite the lighthouse is the **Lady's Rock,** covered by the sea at high tide.

The rock owes its name to the tradition that one of the MacLeans of Duart placed upon it his wife, a daughter of the Earl of Argyll. She was rescued from her perilous situation by fishermen, whom her cries attracted, and then proceeded to her father's castle at Inveraray. Some days later MacLean arrived at Inveraray, in deep mourning. Having sorrowfully told his father-in-law of the mysterious disappearance of his wife, he was surprised to see the door open and the lady present herself before him. He was allowed to leave the castle in safety, but some years afterwards he was slain in Edinburgh by his brother-in-law, Campbell of Calder.

Duart Castle, the seat of the chief of the MacLeans, crowns the nearest prominent point of Mull. It was restored by the 26th chief, Sir Fitzroy MacLean, who died in 1937, aged 101.

A castellated tower near the point is a memorial of *William Black* the novelist (born 1841, died 1898). The site is singularly appropriate, being in the vicinity of the closing scene of one of his most powerful stories, *Macleod of Dare.*

The view from the steamer at this point is one of the finest imaginable. In front are the hills of Kingairloch, Morvern, Ardnamurchan, and Mull. On looking backward, Cruachan is seen towering above the Argyllshire hills. North-eastward are Ben Nevis, the Peaks of Glencoe, and Loch Linnhe, and southward are the Paps of Jura.

Having passed Duart Castle, we are in **The Sound of Mull**. This strait, 2 miles wide and nearly 20 miles long, separates the island of Mull from Morvern on the mainland. In the bay on our left, west of the promontory, is Torosay Castle, and a little beyond that is **Craignure,** terminus of the car-ferry service from Oban. Then the steamer passes over to the Morvern shore. On a projecting rocky site is the shell of the feudal keep of **Ardtornish,** apostrophized in the opening lines of Scott's *Lord of the Isles.* The castle was one of the principal strongholds of the Lords of the Isles—a line of independent or semi-independent chiefs who governed the Western Isles.

Westward of Ardtornish is the mouth of **Loch Aline,** "the beautiful loch," its steep sides picturesquely wooded. It is about 3½ miles long. At its head is **Kinlochaline Tower.**

Some 5 miles west from Lochaline Pier—car ferry connection with Craignure—is the Manse of Fiunary, the home of three generations of clerical Macleods. It was the scene of Norman Macleod's *Reminiscences of a Highland Parish,* and forms the subject of one of the finest of Gaelic songs, *Farewell to Fiunary,* composed by the father of Norman Macleod on becoming parish minister of Campbeltown.

Across the Sound is **Salen** (p. 78). We next pass the ruin of **Aros Castle,** once a residence of the Lords of the Isles, and get a fine view of the saddle-shaped mountains, Ben Talaidh (or Talla) and Ben More (p. 78). Steaming by Drimnin, we glide

into the harbour of **Tobermory** (p. 79), the chief town in the island.

Beyond Tobermory **Loch Sunart,** striking off from the north end of the Sound of Mull, pierces into North Argyll for a distance of 20 miles and separates classic Morvern from the district to the north of Loch Sunart which is called **Ardnamurchan** from the name given to its extremity ("the cape of the great seas"), the most westerly point on the mainland of Scotland—being, indeed, 20 miles west of the meridian of Land's End. Halfway up Loch Sunart is another Salen, and near its head is Strontian (*see* p. 106).

After leaving Tobermory we pass on the Mull side *Bloody Bay*, the scene of a sea-fight between the Macleods and the Macleans in the fifteenth century. On the Ardnamurchan shore just opposite is **Kilchoan** and on its right on the coast the ruins of **Mingary Castle,** where James IV held a court in 1495 and received the submission of the islands chiefs. (Daily—except Sunday—service between Mingary and Tobermory.) Then, rounding **Ardmore Point,** we are on the open waters of the Atlantic.

Far away to the north are visible the islands of **Canna, Rhum, Eigg, and Muck,** and westwards are **Coll** and **Tiree.**

Turning southward, we pass near the **Treshnish Isles,** a ridge of rocky islands extending for 5 miles in a north-easterly direction. One of the group is Bac-Mor, called also, from its shape, "The Dutchman's Cap." Then on the left is the scene of Campbell's poem, *Lord Ullin's Daughter*, if Loch na Keal is "dark Loch Gyle." Anyhow, at its entrance is the island of **Ulva,** with a ferry.

> "Now who be ye would cross Loch Gyle,
> This dark and stormy water?'
> 'Oh, I'm the chief of Ulva's Isle,
> And this, Lord Ullin's daughter.'"

David Livingstone's forebears hailed from this "isle of the wolf."

Loch Tuath separates Ulva from Mull and is connected with **Loch na Keal,** which nearly bisects the island of Mull, there being only some 3 miles between its head and Salen. Lying so close to Ulva as to appear part of it when viewed from the deck of the steamer, is the smaller and less lofty island of **Gometra**. Ulva and Gometra rise respectively to a height of 1,025 and 503 feet, and by some are considered as much worthy of admiration as the Giant's Causeway in Ireland, so impressive are their series of basalt colonnades.

Southward of Ulva and Gometra, **Little Colonsay** is passed. Beyond it and nearer Mull is **Inch Kenneth,** a small green islet on which Dr. Johnson and Boswell enjoyed what the Doctor called the most agreeable Sunday he ever spent, at the cottage of Sir Allan MacLean and his two daughters. An ancient Chapel (which belonged to Iona nuns) and sculptured stones in Inch Kenneth are under the care of the Ministry of Works.

Due west of Inch Kenneth 6 or 7 miles is—

Staffa

"the isle of staves or columns." It is roughly oval in shape and about 2 miles in circumference and is uninhabited. Its length is a mile; its breadth a quarter of a mile. On the south its cliffs rise to a height of 135 feet.

The chief object of interest is **Fingal's Cave,** so named from Fion-na-Gael (Fingal), the great Gaelic hero, whose achievements have been made familiar by the *Fingal* of Macpherson. It is entered by a majestic arch, domed over, and resting on basaltic pillars. The roof rises 60 feet above high-water mark, and the cave penetrates 227 feet into the isle, its width gradually decreasing from 42 feet at the mouth to about 20 feet at its far end. It is very remarkable that this stupendous basaltic grotto remained unknown to the outer world until 1772, when it was visited by Sir Joseph Banks, who, on his way to Iceland, was driven into the Sound of Mull, and there heard from the inhabitants of the great natural wonder.

It was to this cave that Sir Robert Peel referred when he made it his boast that he "had seen the temple not made with hands, had felt the majestic swell of the ocean—the pulsation of the great Atlantic—beating in its inmost sanctuary, and swelling a note of praise nobler far than any that ever pealed from human organ."

The Gaelic name of Fingal's cave—Uamh Binn—means the "musical cave," and has reference to the harmonies called forth by the billows. It inspired Mendelssohn's overture "Die Fingalshöhle" ("Fingal's Cave," or "In the Hebrides"). The composer visited Staffa in 1829.

Terminating in a long projecting point at the eastern side of the great cave is the **Causeway,** also formed of columns. The pillars are for the most part hexagonal, some few are pentagonal, and others have seven, eight, and even nine sides. There is said to be only one square stone on the island—the Corner Stone, as it is called.

The Causeway affords a fine view of the **Bending Pillars,** which present the appearance of being made crooked by the immense weight they support. Half-way along the Causeway is **Fingal's Chair,** a rocky throne said to fulfil the wishes of those who sit in it.

Separated from the Causeway by a narrow channel is **Buchaille,** or the Herdsman, a conical pile of columns rising to the height of 30 feet and forming the first of the series of pillars known as the **Colonnade.**

A staircase at the end of the Causeway gives access to the top of the cliffs, from which is obtained the best view of the **Clam Shell** or **Scallop Cave.** This cannot be entered either by boat or on foot. It is 130 feet long. On one side are basaltic pillars bent like the ribs of a ship; on the other are ends of columns protruding and honeycombed.

A little to the west of Fingal's Cave is the **Boat Cave,** which can be entered only by sea—hence its name. It is a long opening resembling the gallery of a mine, about 16 feet in height, 12 in breadth, and 150 in length. The columns which overhang it, and those in its neighbourhood, are the longest in the island.

The most notable of the many other caves in the island is **Mackinnon's Cave,** alternatively the **Cormorants'** or **Scarts' Cave,** the westernmost of three opening into the south-western face of the cliffs. It is easy of access by a small boat. From the entrance nearly to the end the height is 50 feet and the breadth 48 feet. The cave is 224 feet long, and terminates in a gravelly beach, where a boat may be drawn up. The gloom is so deep in some of its recesses that the movement of the oar excites the phosphorescent gleams of the floating medusæ.

There are the remains of what is believed to have been an ancient Chapel on the island, but today the only sounds heard in its solitudes are the cries of the sea-birds. A floating mine damaged some of the Staffa pillars in the Second World War.

When passing Staffa, steamers are steered as close as possible, to afford passengers an opportunity of viewing the caves and of landing if conditions are favourable.

Standing prominently at the entrance to Loch Scridain, on the coast of Mull, are the ruins of the original of Castle Dare in William Black's novel, *Macleod of Dare*. On the northern shores of Loch Scridain (*see* p. 78) rise the cliffs and heights of the **Ardmeanach** peninsula.

South of Loch Scridain is the long promontory known as the **Ross of Mull,** separated from Iona by the Sound of Iona, less than a mile wide (ferry from Fionphort).

After a voyage of 6 or 7 miles from Staffa, lasting about half an hour, the steamer reaches the sacred island of—

IONA

Access.—*See* p. 80. Steamer passengers are landed and re-embarked in boats. Iona may also be reached by road across Mull (motor-coaches) and Ferry (motor-boat) from Fionphort—the Pilgrims' Way.

Iona was anciently known as I-Chaluim-Chille, "the island of the cell of Columba," the present name being (it is thought) a corruption either of I-thonna ("the island of the waves"), or I-shonna ("the holy or blessed island). But the earliest spelling is Ioua, or simply I, the "island."

Iona, which belongs to the Duke of Argyll, is 3 miles long by 1½ wide. Its shores are marked by low headlands and small bays; but it has no harbour, and the only landing-place is a concrete jetty.

The island first became celebrated through St. Columba crossing over to it from Ireland with twelve companions in the year 563, and founding a monastery from which missionaries went forth to spread the doctrines of Christianity over the adjacent mainland. Iona was afterwards famous as the burial-place of the kings and princes of Scotland, who were influenced in their choice not only by its supposed sanctity, but also by a desire of preserving their remains from the fate awaiting those buried in less favoured spots; for it was foretold that—

> "Seven years before that awful day,
> When time shall be no more,
> A watery deluge will o'er-sweep
> Hibernia's mossy shore;
> The green-clad Islay, too, shall sink,
> While, with the great and good,
> Columba's happy isle shall rear
> Her towers above the flood."

Most literally and completely has been fulfilled the prophecy of Columba before he died (June 9, 597) in his chosen isle. "This place (Iona), small and mean as it appears, shall be honoured not only by the kings of the Scots and their people, but by the rulers of strange nations, and those subject to them. By the holy men also of other churches it shall be held in reverence." Iona today has an aura, an atmosphere, enhanced by indescribably beautiful colour effects.

The monastery erected by Columba was repeatedly destroyed by Norse invaders, and restored again (as by Queen Margaret in the eleventh century). About 1200 it became a Benedictine house. Of a nunnery founded at the same time there remain the chancel, nave, and portions of the vaulted roof of the Chapel, a building of Norman architecture. The charter of the nunnery is one of the treasures of the Vatican. The ruin contains many tombs, the most notable being that of the last prioress, Anna, who died in 1543. St. Ronan's Chapel (now roofed) was the parish church in mediæval times. Preservation work has adorned the cloister garth with a lovely rock garden. West of the Nunnery is the Street of the Dead, leading from the Martyrs' Bay to Reilig Oran (St. Oran's Cemetery), passing the fifteenth-century McLean's Cross, 11 feet high.

Reilig Oran, "the Westminster Abbey of Scotland," has

claims to be the oldest Christian burial-place in Scotland. In it is "gathered together perhaps the most extensive holy alliance or congress of European sovereigns." It is said to contain the graves of forty-eight Scottish, two Irish, one French, and two Norwegian kings, and sundry powerful chieftains and ecclesiastics, but the numbers vary.

According to tradition, the tombs were arranged in nine rows or "ridges," but these can scarcely be distinguished, owing to the levelling influences of time. The kings, it is recorded, were buried in three tombs in the form of small chapels, and were in the third row. The tombs have long since been swept away.

Among the last monarchs buried at Iona was Macbeth (slain in 1057). He was preceded here by Duncan I, whom he murdered in 1040.

> *Ross*—"Where is Duncan's body?"
> *Macduff*—"Carried to Colme's Kil,
>   The sacred storehouse of his predecessors,
>   And guardian of their bones."

In the cemetery is **St. Oran's Chapel,** the most ancient structure in the island, having probably been built by St. Margaret (died 1093), Queen of Malcolm Canmore. Its name is due to the tradition that Columba's disciple Oran was buried alive under the foundation as a sacrifice to the earth god. In the interior is a triple arch said to have formed a canopy to the tomb of St. Oran. It is of later date than the chapel. Other objects of interest include the tomb of Angus Og, who was with Bruce at Bannockburn, and, under the name of Ronald, is Scott's hero in *The Lord of the Isles.*

On approaching the Cathedral we see, opposite the west door, the celebrated **St. Martin's Cross.** It is 14 feet high and 18 inches broad, and is ornamented by sculptured figures, including the Holy Family, David with the harp, and Daniel in the lions' den. It was erected in memory of St. Martin of Tours, and dates from the ninth or tenth century.

Near the west entrance of the Cathedral are the foundations of a small cell or chamber, called **St. Columba's Tomb,** restored in 1955-1956 by the Iona Community. It is pointed out as the burial-place of the Saint and his servant Diarmid, but Ireland claims that the bones of St. Columba were transferred to County Down, while Dunkeld also professes to have received them.

Iona Cathedral

The Abbey Church was dedicated to St. Mary and did not rank as a cathedral until 1506, when Iona became the chief seat of the Bishop of the Isles. In 1899 George, eighth Duke of Argyll, conveyed the ruins to the Church of Scotland, which (by 1910) partly restored or rebuilt the church and fitted it for worship.

The building is 160 feet long by 70 wide. Its erection was begun in the twelfth century, and it is mainly of Norman and Early Pointed architecture, but from the mixture of styles it is evident that it grew, piecemeal, down to the days when, from 1561 onwards, Iona fell a victim to the iconoclastic zeal of the Reformers or to neglect. A square tower. at the intersection of the nave and transept, rises 70 feet, and is supported by four Norman arches and plain cylindrical columns. Some of the capitals are decorated with grotesque figures, still sharp and well preserved. Among the sculptures are representations of the Crucifixion and the Temptation. Another represents an angel weighing souls, while the devil depresses one scale with his claw. The central tomb in the church is that of a Macleod of Macleod. To north and south are effigies of Abbot Mackinnon and Abbot Mackenzie (1500). In the south transept is a marble monument to the eighth Duke of Argyll (1823-1900).

Cloisters were enclosed on three sides by the nave, one of the transepts, and the refectory (restored in 1951). The Monastery was situated behind the Cathedral, and north of the Monastery are the remains of the Bishop's House. Above the Chapter House is the Library (restored). In 1965 the old infirmary of the Abbey was restored and opened. Its restoration was the gift of the

Carnegie Trust. It contains many ancient stones including the remains of St. John's cross and also St. Columba's pillow.

In 1938 was formed the *Iona Community*, its founder being the Very Rev. Dr. George MacLeod. During the summer months successive groups of young ministers, students, and craftsmen are at work under the guidance of architects restoring the monastic buildings to the glory of mediæval times. Gifts of timber and money heve come from Norway, New Zealand, Canada, and the United States, etc. When Queen Elizabeth visited Iona in August 1957—the first British Monarch to do so for 900 years—she witnessed the dedication of the carved oak screen between the nave and the transept, her own gift to the Community.

Rare thirteenth-century silver spoons, a gold fillet and ring were unearthed at the Nunnery in 1923, and in 1950 a hoard of over 300 silver coins dating from the tenth to the eleventh century was brought to light near the north-east end of the Cathedral—presumably part of the Danegeld paid to the Danes in Viking days. A Flemish bell (dated 1540 and found in Sussex) was presented to the Iona Community in 1952, to hang in the Cloisters.

Behind the Cathedral rises **Dun-I** ("the island fortress"), a grey hill, 332 feet high, from the summit of which more than thirty islands may be seen.

Iona contains much that cannot be seen in the time (1¾ hr.) during which the steamer waits. Besides the objects described— and even these cannot be lingered over in pilgrim spirit unless at least a night is spent on the island—there are the **Spouting Cave, Port na Curaich** ("the haven of the Coracle"—the traditional landing-place of St. Columba), **Port Ban** with its lovely white sands, the **Cell of the Culdees,** and the **Marble Quarries.**

The island has a population of about 100, most of whom dwell in the village of *Threld*, or Baile-Mor, "the great city." There are two hotels (unl. *St. Columba, Argyle*) and a golf course. Electricity came to the island in 1957.

Leaving Iona, we steam along the **Ross of Mull** (*see* p. 86), the most southerly part of Mull. The coast abounds with columns of basalt, indented with deep ravines and caves. From the quarries in the Ross was obtained the red granite used in the construction of the Albert Memorial, Blackfriars Bridge, and the Holborn Viaduct, London.

At first we thread our way through the **Torrins, or Torran Rocks,** a dangerous reef which stretches from the neighbourhood of **Erraid Island,** celebrated by "R. L. S.," in *Kidnapped*, half-way to St. John's Rock, 16 miles away, the site of **Dubh Heartach Lighthouse,** visible in clear weather. That lighthouse, by the way, was erected (1867-1872) under conditions of exceptional difficulty. The rock could be approached, on an average, on only fifty days in the year, and was swept by seas so powerful that on one occasion fourteen stones, each weighing two tons, and fixed into the masonry nearly 40 feet above high-water, were torn and swept off the rock.

After clearing the reef, and rounding Ardalanish Point, there comes into view, on the south shore of the Ross, a bold headland called **Gorrie's Head,** or Leap, from a tradition that a retainer called Gorrie, having seized the son and heir of MacLaine of Loch Buie, who caused him to be punished ignominiously for dereliction of duty, leapt from the cliff with the child in his arms, in presence of the distracted father.

Beyond are the **Carsaig Arches,** formed in basaltic rocks by the action of the sea, and very similar to those at Staffa. The larger is 150 feet long, 60 feet high, and 55 feet in breadth. The smaller arch is 70 feet in height, but only a few feet in length. Just eastward of the arches is the **Nun's Cave,** remarkable for carvings believed to be the original designs of the Iona Crosses. The freestone for Iona Cathedral was obtained nearby and sculptured in the cave.

Beyond **Carsaig Bay** we pass—

Loch Buie,

at the head of which are the old and new castles of the Mac-Laines. A small and almost imperceptible hole in the cliffs, at the eastern entrance to the loch, is pointed out as **Lord Lovat's Cave,** and is said to have been one of the hiding-places of that notorious schemer after the battle of Culloden. Also at Loch Buie is to be

91

seen one of the finest examples of Standing Stones or "Druid" Circle. The stones are in a perfect state of preservation. From Loch Buie the steamer shapes its course for the Sound of Kerrera, entering Oban Bay from the side opposite to that of its departure in the morning.

III.—COLL AND TIREE

The islands of Coll and Tiree, west of Mull, can be visited by means of the Inner Islands mail steamer, which leaves Oban at 7 a.m. on Monday, Wednesday, and Friday, and returns early the following morning. There are supplementary sailings in season. By the same steamer one can go on to Castlebay in Barra (*see* p. 154) and to Lochboisdale in South Uist (*see* p. 153).

Coll.—The first stop of the Inner Islands steamer after Tobermory (*see* p. 79) is at **Arinagour** (*hotel*) in Coll, 7 miles west of Mull. Dr. Johnson and Boswell were "stormstayed" here in 1773 and the places at which they stayed can be visited, including the "White House", Capt. McLean's cottage and Breachacha Castle. Next to this castle is the original twelfth-century building, seat of the MacLeans of Coll. Coll is rich in fine beaches, bird life, wild flowers and orchids; the main industry is crofting and farming, producing sheep and beef cattle.

Tiree (pronounced tie-*ree*), 2 or 3 miles to the south-west, has a slightly bigger area (34 square miles) and a much bigger population (1,000) than Coll. Flat and treeless, windswept yet productive, Tiree is rich in archæological interest (ancient Norse forts, standing stones, ruined castle, etc.) and in wild bird life. It offers fishing and bathing and its sunsets and seascapes enthrall the visitor. Tiree (Reef Airport) is connected by air—an hour's flight—with Abbotsinch daily, supplemented in summer, and its port, **Scarinish,** has an hotel.

IV.—TO THE ISLES OF THE SEA

Twice weekly in summer a MacBrayne steamer makes an afternoon cruise to the Isles of the Sea—the Garvelloch group, at the entrance to the Firth of Lorne. These "Holy Isles" may also be viewed at close quarters in the course of the weekly "Six Lochs" excursion, a comprehensive all-day cruise southward to Lochs Melfort, Crinan, and Craignish and back through the swirling Strait of Corryvreckan to Loch Linnhe, Loch Corry (in Morvern), and Loch Creran.

The **Garvellochs,** or **Isles of the Sea,** lie between Jura and Mull at the southern end of the Firth of Lorne, 4 or 5 miles westward of the slate island of Luing (*see* p. 46). The southernmost of the chain, **Eileach an Naoimh** ("Island of the Saints"), or Holy Isle, is associated with the memory of St. Columba. About the middle of its eastern shore are the Saint's landing place and well. Near them, now in custody of the Ministry of Works, are the remains of two beehive cells, of Irish type, the ruins of a chapel, an underground cell, and an old burying-ground with sculptured stones. A little south of the burying-ground is a small stone circle, with a cross rudely engraved on one of the stones. Tradition points to this as the burial-place of St. Columba's mother, Eithne, the island being identified with the Hinba of Adamnan.

Between the most northerly of the group and Luing are the islet of **Belnahua,** all one slate quarry, and **Fladda Lighthouse,** its beams visible for 11 miles. At certain states of the tide the surface of the sea is here covered with countless little whirlpools, miniatures of the famous (or infamous) Corryvreckan to the south.

V.—TO LISMORE AND FORT WILLIAM

Distance.—By steamer from Oban to Fort William, 33 miles, *but see current announcements.*

On Tuesdays and Fridays during the season (late May to mid-September) a MacBrayne Steamer leaves Oban in the morning for Fort William (a 2-hour sail in sheltered waters). It connects there with motor-coaches to and from Inverness by the Great Glen (2¾ hours) and sails for Oban at 2 p.m. On Fridays only a steamer leaves Oban at 6 p.m. for an evening cruise to Fort William and brings back to Oban excursionists by a special day return trip to Inverness. There are also summer evening cruises to Fort William (no landing) on other days.

On leaving Oban pier steamer passengers have on their left the Hutcheson Monument on Kerrera, and on the right Dunollie Castle. After passing Maiden Isle there is a glimpse of Dunstaffnage Castle on the southern shore of Loch Etive, backed by Cruachan in the distance.

On the left is the island of **Lismore,** about 10 miles long and a mile and a half in breadth. (Daily steamers from Oban, except Sundays; ferry to Port Appin.) In olden times Lismore was the seat of the bishops of Argyll, and the cathedral of former days has been converted into the parish church. Robertson described it as "perhaps the humblest cathedral in Britain." Less than 60 feet in length, by 30 in breadth, it has no aisles, and seems to have had neither transepts nor nave. The *Book of the Dean of Lismore*, a sixteenth-century collection of Gaelic and English verse, is of great literary value. (*See also* p. 81.)

The narrow channel between the island and the mainland is the **Lynn of Lorne.** On its right is the entrance to **Loch Creran,** almost blocked by the small island of Eriska.

Then we pass the western extremity of **Airds Bay,** where is a fine natural arch. Shortly afterwards the steamer sails past the tiny village of **Port Appin** (*see* p. 70). On a rocky islet in the main channel of Loch Linnhe stands the roofless ruin of **Castle Stalker** (p. 70).

In front is the larger island of **Shuna,** with another ruined castle. On the mainland is Appin House.

Ardsheal House, frequently visited by Sir Walter Scott in his younger days, looks across the Loch to Glen Tarbert, which separates Morvern from Ardgour.

Then comes **Loch Leven,** a long narrow gulf, presenting to its farthest extremity a succession of grand and romantic landscapes. Near its mouth are *Ballachulish* and the entrance to Glencoe (p. 71).

The steamer sails northwards past the scattered village of **Onich** (*see* p. 102) and enters Upper Loch Linnhe through the Corran Narrows, a favourite defence point in olden times. There is a ferry here and a lighthouse near the western (Ardgour) shore.

A quarter of an hour later we pass on the left, **Inverscaddle Bay,** on the shore of which is Conalglen House, a seat of the Earl of Morton. Ben Nevis appears again on the right, and straight in front is the Great Glen, through which runs the Caledonian Canal (*see* p. 115). A few minutes later the pier at **Fort William** is reached.

FERRIES AT OR NEAR FORT WILLIAM

To Ardgour.—There is a motor-boat ferry (no cars) across Loch Linnhe between Fort William harbour and Camusnagaul in Ardour. *Corran Ferry*, 8½ miles south-west of Fort William, operates 8.15 a.m. (Sunday, 10.30 a.m.) to 7.45 p.m. in summer; 9 a.m.

(Sunday, 10.30 a.m.) to lighting-up time, mid-September to mid-May. Uniform charge for motor cars. Transit between 5 and 10 minutes. State of tide may cause delay.

Ballachulish, 12½ miles down Loch Linnhe from Fort William. The ferry across Loch Leven operates 8 a.m. (Sunday, 9 a.m.) to 9.30 p.m. in summer; 9 a.m. to lighting-up time in winter. Turntable ferry boats. Cars charged according to horse-power (under or over 16 h.p.). Transit 4 or 5 minutes. In case of congestion or other delay motorists may find it preferable to go round Loch Leven by Kinlochleven (*c.* 20 miles). Cars towing caravans or trailers should go round Loch Leven.

OTHER
SCOTTISH GUIDES

IN THIS SERIES

Aberdeen, Deeside, etc.
Edinburgh and District
The Highlands
Glasgow, The Firth of Glyde, the Burns
    Country, etc.
Inverness and Northern Scotland

THE COMPLETE SCOTLAND

A modern and comprehensive volume, describing every road, steamer trip and walking route of importance and with 28 maps and plans.   448 pp.

WARD LOCK LIMITED

Fort William

Access.—*By rail via* Crianlarich (West Highland route); by bus *via* Connel; or by coach from Inverness *via* the Caledonian Canal route; or by coach from Oban.

By road from the south *via* Crianlarich (p. 26), Tyndrum and Glencoe; thence rounding Loch Leven by Kinlochleven; or *via* Connel, where Loch Etive is crossed by the bridge (*see* p. 42) and Ballachulish Ferry (*see* p. 95) or round Loch Leven.

From Perth, etc., *via* Pitlochry and the Great North road to Dalwhinnie, thence by Laggan and Glen Spean. From Inverness *via* the Great Glen and Fort Augustus.

Buses run daily to Onich, North Ballachulish, Kinlochleven, and Ballachulish; Inverlochy and Caol; Corpach; to Fort Augustus and Inverness *via* Spean Bridge; to Roy Bridge (except Sunday); to Glenfinnan (except Sunday); also to Gairlochy, Achnacarry, Kingussie, Glasgow (*via Glencoe*). In the season there are whole day *Coach Tours* to Inverness and round Loch Ness, Glen Affric, etc.; and half-day tours to Glencoe, Glenfinnan, Glen Nevis.

Bowls.—Greens beside the main road at north end of town.

Bus Station.—Near Pier.

Cinema.—*Playhouse* in High Street.

Distances.—London, 524 miles (rail); Edinburgh, 170 (rail); Glasgow, 122 (rail); Oban, 33 by water, 48 by road (*via* Ballachulish Ferry), $67\frac{1}{2}$ *via* Kinlochleven; Inverness, $64\frac{3}{4}$ by road; Fort Augustus, 32; North Ballachulish, 13; Foot of Glencoe (*via* Ballachulish Ferry), 17, (*via* Kinlochleven), 27; Kingussie, 49; Mallaig, 47; Spean Bridge, 10.

Early Closing.—Wednesday (suspended in summer).

Fishing.—Good trouting in the *Nevis* and in numerous other streams and lochs. Permits from local Angling Association and Estate Office of Aluminium Company at Inverlochy. Trout and sea trout fishing on Loch Arkaig (Lochiel Estate). Applications to West Highland Estate Office. Good sea fishing on Lochs Linnhe and Eil.

Golf.—9-hole course.

Hotels.—Among the larger hotels are—*Alexandra* (34 rooms), *Grand* (40), *Highland* (67), *Imperial* (40) *Station* (19), *Croit Anna Motel* (87) (Achintore), *West End* (48), *Cruachan* (14), *Nevis Bank* (10); unl. *Commercial, Berkeley House, Belvedere*, etc.

Information.—Lochaber Tourist Association, Fort William, can give assistance on accommodation and tours, etc. (Tel.: Fort William 2232).

Tobermory Bay, Isle of Mull (*Valentine*)

Loch Etive (*Norward Inglis*)

Iona Cathedral, and St. Oran's Chapel (*Valentine*)

Fort William, and Ben Nevis (*Wm. S. Thomson*)

Museum.—West Highland Museum in Cameron Square, open June-August 9.30-9 p.m., September-May 9.30-5 p.m. *Charge.*
   Scottish Crafts Exhibition in High Street has display of Scottish arts and crafts, largely for sale. *Charge.*

Steamers.—In the season (June to mid-September) a MacBrayne steamer leaves Fort William for Oban at 9 a.m. on Wednesday, on the Iona and Staffa excursion, arriving back at Fort William at 8 p.m. There is also a thrice weekly service to and from Oban.

Tennis.—Courts in Achintore Road.   **Youth Hostel.**—In Glen Nevis.

The town originated in a fort built by General Monk, during the Commonwealth, to overawe the Highlanders and reconstructed in the time of William III, from whom the place derives its name. The fort was unsuccessfully besieged by the Jacobites during the rebellion of 1745, was garrisoned until 1860, and dismantled in 1866. Most of it was levelled after 1894 for the West Highland Railway. The arched gateway (1690) of the fort was re-erected as an entrance to the Craigs burial ground nearby.

Fort William, standing on important rail and road routes, and well equipped for such shipping as still comes this way, is not only a leading tourist centre but also a busy market town, with extending suburbs, distilleries, and the Lochaber works of the British Aluminium Company, which, opened in 1929 and much extended since, are the largest of their kind in Britain. Here, as at the other older plants at Kinlochleven (*see* p. 102) and Foyers,

alumina is reduced to yield aluminium, a process requiring an abundant supply of electricity. The power for generating this is obtained by an extensive system of engineering works whereby the waters of Lochs Treig and Laggan, and even part of the head waters of the Spey, are led through an underground tunnel, the outlet pipes of which can be seen emerging from the northern shoulder of Ben Nevis. The tunnel (15½ miles long) was drilled through solid rock.

The most notable piece of architecture is **St. Andrew's Episcopal Church,** near the north end of the main street. For its size it has few equals in Scotland. The floor of the baptistery and the carvings on the doors are notable. Adjoining it is **The Parade,** with a putting course, a *Statue of Donald Cameron of Lochiel,* twenty-fourth chief of the clan, who died in 1905, and the War Memorial. An interesting possession in the Town Hall is the flag hauled down from Fort William, Calcutta, when the Dominion of India came into being in August 1947. It was presented to the town by Field Marshal Auchinleck. The **West Highland Museum** has a splendid collection of Jacobite relics, tartans, a replica of the interior of a crofter's cottage, and another of the Governor's room at the old Fort in which was signed in 1692 the order for the Massacre of Glencoe (p. 72).

Near the northern exit of Fort William is the old Craigs burial-ground, the gates of which are those of the dismantled fort (*see* p. 97). Beside the entrance is the rock from which the fort was bombarded in 1746. The graveyard contains an obelisk in memory of the Gaelic poet, Ewen MacLachlan (1775-1822).

At the west end of the narrow High Street are the railway station, the pier, several hotels and the bus station. A fine esplanade runs south-westward alongside Loch Linnhe.

Captain Peter Cameron, commander of the celebrated East Indiaman, *The Earl of Balcarres,* is commemorated by an obelisk in the higher portion of the town, which looks out over Loch Linnhe to the Ardgour hills.

About a mile north of Fort William the *Lochy* enters Loch Linnhe. On the south side of the river, near its mouth, is **Old Inverlochy Castle,** a large quadrangular structure with massive round towers at each angle. Of legendary fame, the Castle, now an imposing ruin, was probably erected in the thirteenth century—possibly by Edward I—for the purpose of holding in check the unruly mountaineers. In 1645, at Inverlochy, Montrose completely defeated the first Marquis of Argyll, who retired to a ship at the beginning of the action.

Lochy Bridge, 2 miles north-east of Fort William, leads over to **Caol,** a modern suburb on the bus route to Corpach.

EXCURSIONS FROM FORT WILLIAM

I.—ASCENT OF BEN NEVIS

Time necessary: 5-6 hours. Coaches run to the foot of Ben Nevis in the season. The annual 14-mile Race from Fort William to the Summit and back is won in under 2 hours! This race dates from 1895 and is usually held on the first Saturday in September. There are shelters available to members of the Climbing Societies.

The principal excursion in the neighbourhood is, of course, the ascent of **Ben Nevis** (4,406 feet), the highest mountain in Britain. It is most easily ascended from Achintee Farm (2½ miles from Fort William), which can be reached by motor by *crossing* the Bridge of Nevis at the north end of the town and then turning sharp to the right by a fair road which follows the north bank of the River Nevis. There is a path to the summit (7½ miles from Fort William), but in spite of this there is some stiff climbing to be done after the first mile of so, and strong boots, preferably nailed, are needed on account of the rough rocks. Climbers should carry warm clothing to wear at the top, and sandwiches to eat. The stone building at the summit was from 1883 until 1904 the Scottish Meteorological Society's observatory. Hardy walkers often ascend in the evening and spend the night on the mountain for the sake of the glorious view at sunrise; but mists are apt to cause disappointment.

The name of Ben Nevis has been variously interpreted as meaning the "cloud-capped mountain," the "heaven-kissing hill," and the "hill of heaven," all alluding to the fact that its top is frequently so obscured by clouds and mist as apparently to reach the sky.

From Achintee Farm the path climbs steeply up the hill-side, and at a height of 1,750 feet crosses the south end of the little valley containing Lochan Meall an t-Suidhe. From here it turns sharp to the right, crosses the Red Burn and then rises in steep zig-zags to the summit, which is flat and covered with loose stones of all shapes and sizes. To the south, it slopes away gradually and then very steeply into Glen Nevis. But on the north-east it is cut off by a magnificent range of rock precipices a mile and a half in length and nearly 2,000 feet in height. To the east the summit descends rapidly to a very narrow *arête*, which circles round the head of the glen at the base of the precipice and rises to the summit of Carn Mor Dearg (4,012 feet).

The great north-east precipice is furrowed with many chasms, some of which generally hold snow all the year round. In 1933—and in several summers since then—snow disappeared entirely from the mountain by September, but the records show that snow persisted without a break from 1840 till 1933 and it is probable that this had been going on for centuries.

On a clear day the View from the summit embraces a panorama almost 150 miles in diameter. Nearly all the highest peaks in Scotland are visible and it is claimed that Ireland can be seen, 120 miles away.

"In no other place," Sir Archibald Geikie observes, "is the general and varied character of the Highlands better illustrated, and from none can the geologist, whose eye is open to the changes wrought by subaerial waste on the surface of the country, gain a more vivid insight into their reality and magnitude.

"It is easy to recognize the more marked heights. To the south, away down Loch Linnhe, he can see the hills of Mull and the Paps of Jura closing in the horizon—Loch Eil seems to be at his feet, winding up into the lonely mountains.

"Far over the hills, beyond the head of the loch, he looks across Arisaig and can see the cliffs on the Isle of Eigg, and the dark peaks of Rhum, with the Atlantic gleaming below them. Farther to the north-west, the blue range of the Coolins rises along the skyline, and then sweeping over all the intermediate ground, through Arisaig, and Knoidart, and Clanranald's country (where the Pretender landed, whence also he departed), mountain rises beyond mountain, ridge beyond ridge, cut through by dark glens, and varied here and there with the sheen of lake and tarn.

"Northward runs the mysterious straight line of the Great Glen, with its chain of lochs. Thence to the east and south the same billowy sea of mountain tops stretches out as far as the eye can follow it— the hills and glens of Lochaber, the wide green strath of Spean, the grey corries of Glen Treig and Glen Nevis, the distant sweep of the mountains of Brae Lyon and the Perthshire Highlands, the spires of Glencoe, and thence round again to the blue waters of Loch Linnhe."

A splendid alternative way of reaching the summit—much longer and harder, but perfectly feasible and safe for really strong walkers— is by the Allt a' Mhuillin (pron. *Voolin*) and up the *arête* between Carn Mor Dearg and Ben Nevis. On the north-east precipice there are some of the finest and longest rock climbs in Britain; but they are difficult and for expert climbers only. Full and exact descriptions of these will be found in the Scottish Mountaineering Club's *Guide to Ben Nevis*.

2.—GLEN NEVIS

Glen Nevis, on the southern side of the mountain, is worth exploring; a road goes up the left bank of the river for several miles and there are coach tours in summer.

About 1½ miles from Fort William is a picturesque waterfall called *Roaring Mill*. Further on are the Wishing Stone, a glacial boulder, the Forestry Commission's Nursery and (3 miles from Fort William) the *Glen Nevis Youth Hostel*, a much frequented timber structure (136 beds), beside a bridge across the river. On a height above the Hostel is Dundearduil vitrified fort. Eventually the glen narrows to a grand gorge through which a path leads to **Steall** (9 miles), near the Hut of the Junior Mountaineering Club and some fine waterfalls.

The path may be followed eastwards to the head of Glen Nevis and on to the south end of **Loch Treig**, in the midst of a wild inhospitable area between Rannoch Moor and Glen Spean. From Lochtreighead a rough track leads in 3 miles to Corrour Station, from which the train could be taken back to Fort William, or the route may be reserved. (Loch Ossian Youth Hostel, 20 miles from Glen Nevis Hostel, is a mile east of Corrour station.) From Lochtreighead a track leads through the wild Lairig Leacach (1,685 feet) to Spean Bridge (10 miles).

A pleasant variation in the approach to Glen Nevis is the "Peat Track" route (6 miles) reached by going a mile or so up Lundavra Road from the south end of Fort William. The track, which attains over 700 feet, affords splendid views and leads downward into lower Glen Nevis. It is an enjoyable, if longer, excursion to continue on the old military road to Kinlochleven (about 14 miles) or to leave it at Lochan Lundavra and reach Onich by a track through Glenrigh Forest.

3.—TO GLENCOE

Frequent half-day coach tours during the season. A bus service connects Fort William with North Ballachulish (ferry), Kinlochleven, and Ballachulish. The Fort William-Glasgow coach passes daily through Glencoe.

An excursion to Glencoe should on no account be missed. The road forms part of the grand highway (A82) between Glasgow and Inverness. For the first 8 miles it runs along the eastern side of Upper Loch Linnhe to Corran (*Nether Lochaber Hotel*), where a Ferry (*see* p. 94) plies across the Narrows to Ardgour (*see* p. 105). Attractive little **Onich** (10 miles: *Allt-nan-Ros, Creagdhu, Onich*) looks out over the entrance to Loch Leven. That ardent Celt, the Rev. Alexander Stewart, LL.D., who wrote under the pen-name of "Nether Lochaber," lived in Onich Manse. A couple of miles further on, at **North Ballachulish** (*Loch Leven Hotel*), is the Ferry (*see* p. 94) which obviates the long round to Ballachulish by Kinlochleven, at the head of the loch. This round, nevertheless, by a skilfully engineered road, commanded on one side by the heights of Mamore Forest and on the other by those of Glencoe, offers ample compensation for the expenditure of time and petrol involved by the circuit.

Kinlochleven (21 miles: *Mamore*) has an impressive setting, though the industrial note struck by this upstart town (population 1,800) is apt to jar in such surroundings. Hedged in by romantic mountains, at the mouth of the river *Leven*, it was called into being by the establishment (1909) here of the first important hydro-electric scheme in this country. The Blackwater Reservoir (8 miles long), a few miles to the east, stores the water for the generation of electricity (used for the production of aluminium ingots and carbon electrodes). The dam is 85 feet high and 62 feet thick at the base. In the neighbourhood is an impressive waterfall.

Visitors should make a point of walking three-quarters of a mile along the Old Military Road to the right of the pipe track, for the grand view it opens up. Constructed after the Rebellion of 1745, this long-disused road leads (6 miles) over the mountain ridge (about 1,800 feet) and down by the steep zig-zags of the "Devil's Staircase" into Glencoe at Altnafeadh.

GLEN ROY

On the southern side the road keeps well above the loch.
Halfway between Kinlochleven and **Bridge of Coe** (27 miles)
are the narrows of Caolasnacoan and Corrynakeigh, where Alan
Breck hid immediately after the murder of Campbell of Glenure
in Appin (*see* p. 70). The **Isle of St. Munda,** burial place of the
Macdonalds of Glencoe, lies off the entrance to **Glencoe,** of
which a full description will be found on pp. 71-4.

4.—THE PARALLEL ROADS OF GLEN ROY

These can be approached by rail or road (bus) from Fort William to Roy
Bridge (13 miles). They begin about 2 miles north of that, and extend to
Brae Roy Shooting Lodge (10 miles), to which there is a road. An excellent
view of them is obtained from a point about midway. Beyond the Lodge a
track (10 miles) climbs up the Glen to over 1,300 feet, above little Loch
Spey, then drops to join the Corrieyairack Pass (*see* p. 119) at Drummin
(Melgarve).

The Parallel Roads are shelves or terraces formed by the waters
of a lake that once filled the intervening glen. The highest (1,155
feet above sea-level) is, of course, the oldest, and those below it
(at 1,077 and 862 feet) were formed in succession as the waters
of the lake decreased in depth. The lake not only filled Glen Roy,
but also some of the valleys adjoining it on the west. The water
was held by a glacier in the glen and in the Great Glen. The latter
was apparently filled with ice, which blocked the mouths of
Glens Roy and Spean. Parallel Roads are also to be seen in
Glen Gloy and lower Glen Spean.

Long before scientists discovered the origin of the "roads,"
the Highlanders accounted for them to their own satisfaction.
They declared that the terraces were hunting walks, cut by the
Picts for their kings, who held court at Inverlochy Castle.

Road and railway pass within a short distance of the old
castle and then by the famous **Ben Nevis Distillery,** which sends
forth that brand of whisky known as "Long John." There
presently appears on the left the modern **Inverlochy Castle.**
Farther on, also on the left, a series of sheds and the hardy
cattle of a Highland ranch catch the eye. Nine miles from Fort
William we reach **Spean Bridge** (*Spean Bridge*; unl. *Druiman-
darrich*). General Wade's military road crossed the *Spean* lower

103

down at High Bridge, now a ruin, where took place the first skirmish of the Rebellion of 1745.

The branch line from Spean Bridge to Fort Augustus is derelict, a bus service taking its place. The West Highland Line and our road now leave the Great Glen for the valley of the Spean. Beyond the three-span bridge, the Fort Augustus road swings round to the left, mounts steadily for a mile and at its junction with a road down to Gairlochy passes the impressive **Memorial to the Commandos**, who trained at Achnacarry. The work of Scott Sutherland, it was unveiled in 1952 by the Queen Mother. At Spean Bridge, however, we take the road to the right, pass **Inverroy**, a Highland clachan, and reach **Roy Bridge** (*Roy Bridge, Glenspean Lodge*) at the mouth of Glen Roy.

A mile or two past Roy Bridge, on the road to Laggan and Kingussie, the Spean surges down the magnificent **Monessie Falls.**

5.—TO ACHNACARRY

Buses make a circular trip embracing Achnacarry and Gairlochy, the surging Falls of Mucomir, the Commandos Memorial, and Spean Bridge.

The Mallaig road (p. 106) is followed as far as Banavie (where passengers used to embark and disembark in the days of the Caledonian Canal steamers). From Banavie (*hotel*), which enjoys an impressive full-length view of Ben Nevis, the Achnacarry road runs along the west side of the Canal and (on a lower level) the river Lochy. Down a side road, a mile or two from Banavie, are the remains of the so-called Banquo's House, or **Tor Castle.** An ancient seat of the Mackintosh chiefs, it stands on a lofty precipice overhanging the Lochy. (A pleasant round can be enjoyed by taking the Corpach bus to Banavie, proceeding on foot thus far by road, and returing to Banavie by the Canal path.) Farther along the Achnacarry road, on the left, is Glen Loy. This beautiful glen penetrates the fastnesses of Locheil country and communicates by path with Glen Suileag, which runs down to Loch Eil. At Gairlochy, locks lead into Loch Lochy, 10 miles long by a mile wide, with mountain guardians on both sides.

Here strikes off the road to Spean Bridge, about a mile along which is the dam built on the site of the former Falls of Mucomir holding back water from the Spean before it joins the river Lochy. (This Gairlochy road joins the main road to Inverness at the Commandos Memorial—*see* p. 104—and enables motorists to combine excursions 4 and 5).

Achnacarry (15 miles from Fort William) is a manor house, the home of the Camerons of Lochiel, at the foot of Loch Arkaig, a narrow sheet of water (12 miles long) connected with Loch Lochy by the river Arkaig. Near the site stood the old castle of the Lochiels which was burnt by the Duke of Cumberland in 1746, and of which only a fragment remains. Close to Achnacarry House along the banks of the Arkaig river is the beech avenue planted by the Gentle Lochiel before he set out for the Forty-Five. It is now sadly thinned by old age and gales. The public road from Clunes, on Loch Lochy, to the foot of Loch Arkaig runs through a pass between wooded hills and this is known as the "Dark Mile"; above the dam at the west end of this road is a cave in which "bonnie Prince Charlie" hid in his flight from Culloden. Beside Loch Arkaig was hidden the famous "treasure"—27,000 louis d'or from France which came too late to help the Rebellion of 1745—the root of so much Jacobite intrigue and romance.

6.—TO ARDGOUR AND ACHARACLE

Cross by the Camusnagaul ferry (*see* p. 94) at Fort William, then take the southward road along Loch Linnhe, from which a magnificent view of Ben Nevis is obtained. Two-thirds of the way along the route the bay at the opening to Cona Glen and Glen Scaddle is rounded; thereafter the loch-side is skirted to Corran Ferry, 11 miles from Camusnagaul. (Bus back to Fort William along the east side of Loch Linnhe.)

The mountainous district of Ardgour is circled in the course of the Loch Shiel Tour (*see* p. 107).

From the head of Loch Eil (14 miles from Fort William) a road (A861) goes down the south side of the loch and along the west shore of Loch Linnhe past Corran Ferry (22 miles from

Kinlocheil). It offers a superb view of Loch Leven and the Glencoe mountains before turning up **Glen Tarbert,** whose austerity is being relieved by afforestation. Soon after reaching the end of long **Loch Sunart** we come to **Strontian** (15 miles from Corran Ferry: *hotel*) which gave its name—it is pronounced Stron-*tee*-an—to Strontium. The mineral strontianite was first found in lead mines here in 1790.

To **Salen** (*hotel*), 10 miles along Loch Sunart, the road is charmingly fringed with oaks and birches. At Salen we swing north for **Acharacle** (*hotel*: 27 miles from Corran) at the foot of Loch Shiel and midway between Loch Sunart and **Loch Moidart,** whose entrance is guarded by the island of Shona. Acharacle is connected by boat with Glenfinnan and by bus (*via* Salen) with Corran and also with Kilchoan (*see* p. 83) in Ardnamurchan.

7.—TO GLENFINNAN· ARISAIG, MORAR AND MALLAIG

All these can be visited by road or by rail. By the West Highland Line (observation cars), Mallaig is 42 miles from Fort William; by road (A830) it is 47 miles. Nearly all the way they run side by side. For the most part the road is narrow (with passing bays) and its numerous twists and sharp gradients call for caution on the part of drivers. Heavy lorry traffic does not improve the surface. To Glenfinnan a bus runs on several weekdays and in the season there are coach tours on Thursdays and Sundays.

The route us through a region of surpassing beauty, enhanced by romantic memories of the Forty-Five, the region where Prince Charles landed on the Scottish mainland and where, after Culloden sealed the failure of his attempt to restore the Stewarts to the throne, he re-embarked for France, "a sair, sair altered man."

The road skirts the shore of Loch Linnhe, crosses the Lochy and Corpach Moss, and enters Banavie, from which it goes on to Corpach (*hotel*), which commands a superb view of Ben Nevis. A little beyond Corpach we pass **Killmallie Church,** in front of which is an obelisk to the memory of Colonel John Cameron of Fassifern, who fell at Quatre Bras, 1815. The epitaph was written by Sir Walter Scott. To the left of this monument an Iona Cross marks the grave of the Gaelic poetess, Mary Mackellar (*née* Cameron: 1834-1890). Beyond **Annat,** road and rail run close to the shore of **Loch Eil** (*Achdalieu:* fishing and shooting), the scene of a memorable fight in which Sir Ewen Cameron of Lochiel, "the Ulysses of the Highlands" as Macaulay calls him, was so hard pressed by an officer of General Monk's garrison that he only succeeded in escaping by planting his teeth in the officer's throat.

Near the centre of the north side of the Loch is **Fassifern House,** the birthplace of Colonel John Cameron and connected with Prince Charlie, who spent a night under its roof. At the head of the loch is **Locheilside,** a district known also as Kinlocheil. Here it was that the Prince heard the Government had offered a reward of £30,000 for his capture, a proclamation to which he replied by another offering a like sum (originally he proposed £30) for the capture of the "usurper," George II.

Crossing the *Fionn Lighe* (the white stream) we have on the right a green hillock, known as **Druim na Saille,** on which large quantities of fish were prepared and salted for shipment to France and Spain in the days when Loch Eil was a famous fishing ground. After traversing the strath stretching westwards from the head of Loch Eil we pass through **Glen Callop** to **Loch Shiel,** a freshwater lake some 18 miles in length, and every-where less than a mile in width. There is no road along either side. About 7 miles away on the west shore of the Loch is **Glenaladale House,** the old family residence of the MacDonalds and the resting-place of Prince Charles for one night after Culloden. In narrows 6 miles further down St. Finnan's Isle has a ruined chapel and an ancient burial ground.

Fishing in the loch is available to visitors at the hotel known by the old name of the *Stage House*, at the head of the Loch, and at *Loch Shiel Hotel*, at **Acharacle** (*see* p. 106) at its foot.

Loch Shiel Circular Tour.—A delightful round-trip from Fort William takes one by motor-coach to Glenfinnan and Loch Shiel, by motor vessel down the Loch to Acharacle, and thence by coach to Salen, along the northern shore of lovely Loch Sunart, through Strontian (*see* p. 106) and the wild scenery of Glen Tarbert to the shore of Loch Linnhe, which is crossed at Corran Ferry (p. 95). This entrancing trip can also be made in the reverse order.

Northward from Loch Shiel is seen historic **Glenfinnan,** with the viaduct which carries the railway over the valley. The great structure is one of the engineering triumphs of the line. It is

1,248 feet in length, and the arches rise in the centre to a height of 110 feet.

By the head of Loch Shiel is the **Glenfinnan Monument,** a column surmounted by a statue of a Highlander. It marks the spot where Prince Charlie's ill-fated standard —of red silk with a white centre—was unfurled. The inscription on the monument is in English, Gaelic, and Latin. The English version runs—

"On the spot where Prince Charles Edward first raised his standard on the 19th day of August, 1745, when he made the daring and romantic attempt to recover a throne lost by the imprudence of his ancestors, this column was erected by Alexander MacDonald, Esq., of Glenaladale, to commemorate the generous zeal, the undaunted bravery and the inviolable fidelity of his forefathers and the rest of those who fought and bled in that arduous and unfortunate enterprise. The pillar is now, alas! also become the monument of its amiable and accomplished founder, who, before it was finished, died in Edinburgh on the 4th day of January 1815, at the early age of twenty-eight years."

The Monument belongs to the National Trust for Scotland.

From Glenfinnan road and rail pass through a winding, narrow valley to **Loch Eilt,** a freshwater loch dotted with islets. We reach the sea again at the head of **Loch Ailort** (*hotel*) and soon enjoy a magnificent view of **Loch nan Uamh** (Loch of the Caves: pronounced *oo'ar*), with its rock-bound shores. Far out in the ocean is the island of Eigg, with the mountains of Rhum on its right, and Muck on its left. It was in Loch nan Uamh at Borrodale that the French frigate *Doutelle* anchored on July 19, 1745, and six days later Prince Charles Edward landed with the "Seven Men of Moidart."

Borrodale is a region associated with the final wanderings of Prince Charlie. After Culloden, he fled to Glen Beasdale, where he waited till a boat could be obtained to convey him to the Outer Isles, hoping to find a ship there that would carry him to France. But from South Uist he returned to the mainland, piloted part of the way by Flora Macdonald. He landed near Mallaig, made his way to Borrodale, and was thence conducted through the military cordon to the friends who hid inland among the hills and caves. At last (September 20, 1746) from Borrodale he stepped on board the ship which carried him and a large company of followers to France.

Proceeding over a low-lying moss and crossing the *Brunery Burn*, we reach **Arisaig** (*hotel*), a hamlet at a charming spot. The coast is studded with rocks, on which seals may be seen in large numbers on a calm summer day, and the view includes Loch nan Cilltean, with its countless rocks and islets. There is boating, bathing, and fishing, but perhaps the most attractive feature of Arisaig as a holiday resort is the variety of little coves and bays within easy reach—all well worth exploring. **Loch nan Cilltean** was visited by two French frigates in the April after Culloden, with arms and treasure to rally once more the scattered champions of the Stewarts. They were attacked by three British frigates, which fought until their ammunition was exhausted and then had to make for the open sea, over which they were chased "for about a league."

Beyond Arisaig we come suddenly upon a series of indescribably beautiful views over land and water. For the next 4 or 5 miles the route runs over the Arisaig peat moss at the base of the Morar hills. From Morar Bridge there is a glimpse of **Loch Morar,** the deepest lake in Great Britain (987 feet). On one of its many islands Simon Lord Lovat took refuge in 1746, and there he was taken captive. The loch contains salmon, sea-trout,

and loch-trout (fishing free to residents of the *Morar Hotel*)—
not to mention a legendary monster. At the falls on the Morar
River a small hydro-electric scheme, supplying power to surrounding districts, has its station commendably hidden in the hill-
side. That portion of the river to the west of the road and railway
is flanked by expanses of pure white sand.

Mallaig

Mallaig is a small town (population 900) busy with fishing and
shipping, with gorgeous views across the Sound of Sleat to
Skye. During the fishing season dozens of steam drifters may be
seen in its harbour, where their freights are landed for dispatch
to southern markets. Mallaig (*West Highland*, *Marine* and board
residence) is a splendid centre for boating excursions along this
rocky, indented coast. Inland there are fascinating excursions
beside or upon Loch Morar and Loch Nevis and about the
intervening hills. Buses connect Mallaig daily (except Sunday)
with Morar and Arisaig.

Mallaig offers exceptional facilities for visiting other ports. New car-
ferry services daily (except Sunday) to Skye (crossing to Armadale in
30 minutes), to Kyle of Lochalsh, and Stornoway (Lewis); and also serve
Eigg, Rhum, Canna, Lochboisdale (South Uist), Loch Maddy (North
Uist), Tarbert, and other ports in Harris. Once a week, in connection
with trains from and to Fort William, a steamer goes to Loch Scavaig
on the south coast of Skye, where (weather permitting) passengers are
taken ashore and given the opportunity of seeing Loch Coruisk. There
is also (on certain days) a motor-boat service to Loch Nevis which is
very handy for walkers, who can land at Tarbert Bay and walk back
by the north shore of Loch Morar (good path) to Morar, or vice
versa. Circular cruises (Loch Nevis and Loch Morar) are available in
the season. For the ferry to Armadale in Skye *see* p. 129. *See also local
timetables.*

TO EIGG, RHUM, AND CANNA

Belonging to the Inner Hebrides, the islands of Eigg, Rhum, and Canna
are served by the Inshore Mail Service from Mallaig, *but see local timetables.*

Eigg, Rhum and Muck are flippantly called the "Cocktail

Islands," but the absence of hotels and infrequent transport do not encourage guests. Nevertheless they repay a visit.

Eigg (pronounced *egg*) lies 7 miles west of the nearest point of Arisaig. About 5 miles long, it owes its striking outline to the basaltic **Scuir** (1,289 feet) in the south, a feature described by Hugh Miller as "a tower three hundred feet in breadth, by four hundred and seventy feet in height, perched on the apex of a pyramid, like a statue on a pedestal."

The island has remarkable caverns. One of these, the **Cave of St. Francis,** was the scene of the ruthless massacre of the inhabitants by the vengeful Macleods of Skye about the end of the sixteenth century, some two hundred hapless Macdonalds being smothered to death in their place of refuge. Human remains found in the cave help to bear out the story. Laig Bay, on the western shore, presents magnificent cliffs and its white sands emit musical sounds when disturbed. The port is in the south-eastern corner The inhabitants, crofters and fishermen, have dwindled to little over a hundred—a fifth of the total in 1851.

The tiny island of **Muck**, 3 miles to the south-west, is occupied by sheep and half a dozen families. Its unromantic name may be a corruption of Monk's island—it once belonged to the Culdess of Iona. More probably Muck is derived from Gaelic *muic*, pig or boar—perhaps from its shape.

Rhum, 4 or 5 miles north-west of Eigg, and nearly four times its size (42 square miles as against 12), is distinguished by its lofty hills rising abruptly from the shore. **Askival** (2,659 ft.) is the highest of a cluster of peaks at its southern end. At the head of Loch Scresort, in the north-east, stands Kinloch Castle, built by the former owner of the island, Sir George Bullough. Hundreds of deer graze on the steep slopes and wild goats roam the high pastures. Long the "Forbidden Island," Rhum was acquired by the Nature Conservancy in 1957. The Loch Scresort area is now open to the public; elsewhere access is subject to restrictions in the interest of research work.

Canna, 3 miles north-west of Rhum and about a tenth its area, is famed for its **Compass Hill,** which contains so much magnetic iron ore that the compasses of passing vesssls are affected. The

Harbour is also at the east end, sheltered by the adjacent islet of Sanday. Canna means cotton-grass. The mild climate is witnessed by its wild flowers and early vegetables.

MALLAIG TO KYLE BY STEAMER

For the direct steamer service and other connections, see local timetables (MacBrayne).

The steamer on its way to Kyle of Lochalsh passes through the **Sound of Sleat** between Skye and the mainland. On each side of the Sound is superb mountain scenery. On the left are the **Sleat Hills** (rising at the north end to roughly 2,400 feet), while the mainland abounds with mountains of even greater elevation and of marked outline. Here, too, are long arms of the sea—Loch Nevis and Loch Hourn ("the loch of heaven" and "the loch of hell"), to the south and north of **Knoydart** respectively.

Four miles beyond Armadale we pass the ivy-covered ruins of **Knock Castle,** with the clachan of Teangue (pronounced as *tongue*) on the shores of a shallow bay. We next approach **Isle Ornsay** (St. Oran's Isle), the site of a lighthouse important in the navigation of the channel. The village (*see* p. 135) comes into sight, together with the Duisdale Hotel, occupying a pleasand situation on the craggy shore.

On the opposite coast is the wild and gloomy **Loch Hourn,** stretching inland for about 15 miles through a series of fine mountains, the nearest and most outstanding being Ben Screel (3,196 feet).

On the eastern side of the Sound of Sleat the steamer passes **Glenelg**, a neat little village. Glenelg Youth Hostel was formerly a ferry inn, occupying the site of the hostelry where Dr. Johnson and Boswell fared so miserably and quarrelled so dramatically. Here at the head of the Sound of Sleat the steamer enters the narrow **Kyle Rhea** ("the king's strait"), at the mouth of which is a ferry, which for ages was the chief means of communication between Skye and the mainland at Bernera. On the right of the Kyle is the "dyke" (stone wal) marking the boundary between Inverness-shire and Ross-shire.

Sligachan Hotel, and Glen Sligachan, Skye (*Wm. S. Thomson*)

The Coolins of Skye, from Elgol (*Alasdair Alpin MacGregor*)

Loch Ness and Loch Oich (*W. S. Thomson*)

Loch Maree (*W. A. Sharp*)

Loch Alsh extends inland for about 5 miles, and then branches, forming **Loch Long** to the north-east and **Loch Duich** to the south-east. The latter, hemmed in by steep mountains—the "Five Sisters of Kintail"—offers the finest scenery of the district. Scour Ouran (3,505 feet) and Ben Attow (3,383 feet) tower at the head of Loch Duich (*see* p. 120).

On the northern coast of Loch Alsh is **Balmacara,** where the small hamlet of Reraig (hill behind, Sgurr Mhor, 1,200 ft.) comes into view with *Balmacara Hotel*, whose picturesque loch-side situation attracts many visitors. Towards Kyle Balmacara House (used for a boys' residential school specializing in rural education) is a conspicuous landmark. On an eminence near the shore is a monument erected by Sir Robert Murchison, the geologist, to commemorate the virtues of an ancestor, Donald Murchison, factor of the Earl of Seaforth—MacKenzie of Kintail—at the time of the rebellion of 1745. In defiance of the English, he for ten years collected the rents on the confiscated Seaforth estates and transmitted them to the Earl, who had fled to Spain. His faithful services, however, were ill-requited when the Earl returned; Donald was treated with coldness and neglect and died of a broken heart.

To the voyager Loch Alsh is apparently land-locked, but egress is obtained westward through a narrow strait named **Kyle Akin,** after the Norwegian king Haco, who sailed through it in 1263. On the Skye shore are the ruins of **Castle Moyle** and **Kyleakin** (*see* p. 131), displaying some of the finest landscapes in the Western Highlands. The hill behind the village is **Beinn na Caillich**—"the old woman's hill" (2,396 feet). The ferry ($\frac{1}{2}$ mile) between Kyleakin and Kyle of Lochalsh opposite is today the chief connecting link for traffic between Skye and the mainland (*see* p. 129).

Kyle of Lochalsh

The western terminus of the line from Dingwall (*see* p. 13) and of highroads from the west and the south (*see* p. 18), the "Gateway to Skye" and a departure point of steamer services to Stornoway, Kyle of Lochalsh (*Lochalsh*, *Kyle*) is an obvious holiday centre, with banks and shops (half holiday Thursday), deep-sea fishing, and boating, and a choice of alluring excursions by land and sea—cruises to Loch Duich and other lochs, and motor tours through Skye. Buses connect the village with neighbouring beauty spots—Plockton, Balmacara, and Glenshiel, and on certain days with Inverness.

From Kyle of Lochalsh there are regular steamer services (daily except Sunday) to Mallaig; to Stornoway; and several times a week to Skye. MacBrayne's time-tables should be consulted. A vessel sails every afternoon (except Sunday) to Loch Toscaig, south of Applecross, and a vessel links Kyle with Kylerhea three times a week.

The Outer Isles are accessible by crossing from Kyle to Kyleakin (ferry), across Skye to Uig (coach), and car ferry to Tarbert in Harris and Loch-maddy in North Uist.

The Great Glen

Motoring.—A road (A82) runs through the Glen all the way from Fort William to Inverness (66½ miles). Formerly dangerous and difficult, it is now a magnificent highway. The first stretch keeps well to the east of the canal, *via* Spean Bridge, from which the road turns north to the eastern shore of Loch Lochy, which is followed as far as Laggan Locks (21 miles from Fort William); thence, with the exception of a short stretch between Loch Oich and Fort Augustus, the main road runs along the western bank.

There is a regular daily bus service all the year round between Fort William and Inverness, *via* Spean Bridge (where it connects with trains from and to the South) and Fort Augustus.

The **Great Glen** is a deep natural depression extending north-eastwards across Scotland from Fort William to Inverness, from Loch Linnhe, or the Firth of Lorne, to the Moray Firth. In recent years there has been extensive planting and development by the Forestry Commission. The Glen provides the route of **The Caledonian Canal.**

The construction of the Canal was begun in 1804 under Telford. Much trouble was caused by the numerous rapid burns flowing from the west into the Lochy. Sluices had to be constructed through the solid rock to convey these waters under the Canal to the river, and the bed of the Lochy had to be raised 12 feet to cause that stream to fall into the Spean at Mucomir. But the greatest difficulty arose in connecting Loch Lochy with the sea at Corpach. The distance between the two points is only 8 miles, but the surface of the lake is 93 feet above sea-level. Telford overcame the difficulty by constructing a series of locks, eight close together (each with a drop of 8 feet) at Banavie being known as **Neptune's Staircase.** Altogether there are twenty-nine locks on the Canal.

The Canal was opened for traffic in 1822, but the passage was soon found to be almost useless. Then improvements were effected, and the Canal was

re-opened in 1847. The cost to the nation, to which it belongs, exceeded a million and a quarter.

The total length of the passage from Corpach to Muirtown (Inverness) is 60½ miles, of which only 22 miles are canal (20 feet deep, 50 feet broad at the bottom, and taking vessels with draught not exceeding 14 feet). The portions of the natural waterway are Loch Lochy (10 miles), Loch Oich (4 miles), and Loch Ness (24 miles).

The southernmost section of the Canal, between Loch Linnhe and Loch Lochy, has already been described (*see* p. 104). The main highway to Inverness (A82) crosses the Spean at Spean Bridge, climbs westward to the Commandos Memorial and then, following the line of one of Wade's military roads, runs north to the east shore of Loch Lochy, passing Glenfintaig Lodge and Invergloy, at the mouth of **Glen Gloy,** which has a "parallel road" slightly higher than the highest in Glen Roy.

At the northern end of the loch, near **Kinloch Lochy,** at the foot of **Ben Tee** (2,957 feet), a fierce clan battle was fought between the Frasers and a branch of the MacDonalds on a hot July day in 1544. It obtained the name of *Blar-nan-Leine*, the "Battle of the Shirts," because the combatants stripped for action.

The **Laggan Locks** lead into a short section of canal between Lochs Lochy and Oich. Here are a Youth Hostel (formerly an hotel) and the old burying-place of **Kilfinnan,** where amid the dust of his ancestors, were laid to rest the mortal remains of Alastair McDonell of Glengarry, the last example of the old-school Highland Chieftain, a friend of Sir Walter Scott's and supposed to be the prototype of Fergus MacIvor in *Waverley*. A swingbridge carries the main road across the Canal at this end of **Loch Oich,** a beautiful loch about 4 miles long. It forms the summit level of the Canal (105 feet). Beside the road near the southern end of the loch is a strange monument overlooking a spring (now beneath the roadway) called *Tobar nan Ceann*— **The Well of the Heads.** The monument consists of a pyramid surmounted by seven human heads carved in stone, and bears in English, Gaelic, French, and Latin the following inscription (which is inaccurate, historically, on more points than one)—

As a Memorial of the ample and summary vengeance which, in the swift course of Feudal Justice, inflicted by the orders of the Lord McDonell and Aross, overtook the perpetrators of the foul murder of the Keppoch family, a branch of the powerful and illustrious Clan of which his Lordship was the Chief, this monument is erected by Colonel McDonell of Glengarry, XVII Mac-mhic Alistair, his Successor and Representative, in the year of our Lord 1812.

The heads of the seven murderers were presented at the feet of the Noble Chief in Glengarry Castle, after having been washed in this spring; and ever since that event, which took place early in the sixteenth century, it has been known by the name of "Tobar-nan-Ceann," or "The Well of Heads."

In the middle of the west side of Loch Oich lies **Invergarry,** at the mouth of Glen Garry. Invergarry (*hotels*: angling in loch and rivers) is 25 miles from Fort William, 41 from Inverness. On a rocky headland called Creagan Fhithich (the "Rock of the Raven": a name adopted as their war-cry by the McDonells of Glengarry), stands the ruins of the ancient **Invergarry Castle,** long the home of the chiefs of the clan. Prince Charles Edward spent part of the night of August 26, 1745, within its walls, just before he started on his journey south, and he also took shelter in it the first night after the battle of Culloden, although it was then deserted. A few days later it was laid in ruins by the Duke of Cumberland. To the right of the old stronghold is the former mansion, now the *Glengarry Castle Hotel*. Of interest in Invergarry is a salmon hatchery run by the North of Scotland Hydro-Electric Board (*visitors welcome*).

The *River Garry* flows through a glen of great grandeur and beauty. The well-known bonnet got its name from the Glengarry Fencibles.

Invergarry to the West Coast.—Motorists bound for Kyle of Lochalsh and Skye may leave the main Fort William-Inverness road at Invergarry. The first portion (by A87) is through woods and for about 2 miles along the north side of **Loch Garry** (at far west end of Loch is *Tomdoun Hotel*, with salmon and trout fishing). The road then strikes north over by the foot of Loch Loyne to meet the Glen Moriston road below the east end of Loch Cluanie. The road then turns westward and skirts the north side of Loch Cluanie to *Cluanie Inn* (21 miles from Invergarry). The remainder of the route to Kyle of Lochalsh is as described on p. 120.

The Glen Garry and Glen Moriston hydro-electric schemes, based on a drainage area of 300 square miles, have involved considerable damming and road reconstruction.

From Tomdoun a road keeps up the Garry valley to **Loch Quoich**—which boasts the largest rockfill dam in Britain: 1,000 feet long, 120 feet high—and ends at the head of **Loch Hourn.** The descent to Kinlochhourn (27 miles from Invergarry: no hotel) is dangerously steep. For Loch Hourn *see* also p. 112.

Fort Augustus

Angling.—In *Loch Ness* and in *Loch Tarff*, 4 miles distant. The former is open to guests at the hotels. For salmon it is nearly as good in spring as Loch Tay, and trout are abundant. Loch Tarff contains trout and char.

Caravans and Camping.—At west end of village.

Golf.—9-hole course.

Hotels.—*Lovat Arms, Caledonian, Inchnacardoch, White Gates.*

Pony Trekking.—From Inchnacardoch Hotel.

Fort Augustus (originally Kilcumein) stands at the head of Loch Ness, at a spot where the Canal and the mouths of the *Oich* and the *Tarff* (the two chief feeders of the loch) are close together. The Fort which gave its name to the town was built after the supression of the Rebellion of 1715. Here Lord Lovat was held a prisoner until he could be taken to London for execution; and to the Fort was brought the bleeding head of Roderick Mackenzie, a young Edinburgh lawyer, and delivered to the Duke of Cumberland as the head of Prince Charles Edward. Fort Augustus was visited by Dr. Johnson and Boswell in 1773 when on their way to Skye. In 1867 the Fort was sold to the Lord Lovat of that day, and in 1876 his son presented the site to the Benedictine order of monks for the erection of a monastery, soon raised to the dignity of an abbey. The ecclesiastical buildings that have been erected within and about the fort, much of which has been incorporated with them, form an imposing pile in the Early English style. The Abbey School is well known. Visitors are permitted to enter the museum. Fort Augustus is a pleasant township, through the centre of which the Canal steps its way. There are good hotels. The rail connection with Spean Bridge is a thing of the past, a bus service (22 miles) taking its place.

From Fort Augustus there runs south-eastwards a Wade road, well-known to walkers as the **Corrieyairack Pass** (2,507 feet). It leads to the Spey at Garva Bridge, and to Laggan (25 miles), which is 8 miles from the Highland line at Dalwhinnie or at Newtonmore. The track is a stern test for walkers, though it has not daunted the striding pylons of the electric grid; throughout the 25 miles there are no inns or shelters.

Loch Ness

Loch Ness, facing Fort Augustus, is the second largest loch in Scotland; it is 22½ miles long, from 1 to 1½ wide and famed, among other things, for the "monster" which is reputed to live in its depths. In spite of no small amount of "eye-witness testimony," including photographs, the sceptics are not yet convinced, and from time to time scientific attempts are made to solve the problem. Owing to the great depth of the loch (745 feet) its surface never freezes. The scenery along its shores is magnificent. On both sides are mountains, which recede somewhat at the northern end and are luxuriantly clothed with trees and copsewood.

A good road leads off to the east of Loch Ness, climbing steeply up romantic **Glen Doe** and past Loch Tarff to **Whitebridge** (9 miles; *hotel*, with fishing; bus to Inverness). From Whitebridge the road (A862) to Inverness (25 miles) keeps high above the level of Loch Ness by Loch Mhor, with glorious views of the mountains both east (the Monadhliaths) and west, but one can go sharply down to **Foyers** (*hotel*)—the famous Falls have lost some of their appeal owing to the works of the British Aluminium Company—and skirt Loch Ness by Inverfarigaig to Dores.

West Side of Loch Ness.—The main highway (A82) takes the west side, and from Fort Augustus to the outskirts of Inverness presents a model of up-to-date road engineering.

Six miles from Fort Augustus is **Invermoriston.** The hotel and the few houses which form the village are nearly a mile from the pier (*camping site*). A fine view of the falls on the *Moriston* can be had from the summer-house by the bridge.

The village is close to the mouth of the *Moriston*, a brawling, cascading river 19 miles long. In the mountains to the west, Lochs Cluanie and Loyne, the two natural reservoirs of the river, form the basis of the Glen Moriston hydro-electric scheme. The "Seven Men of Glenmoriston," outlaws themselves, faith-

119

fully guarded and guided the fugitive Prince Charles for three weeks in August 1746.

Invermoriston to Glenelg and Kyle of Lochalsh (56 miles). This road (A887)—one of the highways to Skye: used by Johnson and Boswell in 1773—lies through woods and along the north bank of the river Moriston, and has been reconstructed. At Dundreggan are a reservoir and an underground generating station. The road skirts **Loch Cluanie**, the raising of whose level necessitated a new section from Cluanie Dam to *Cluanie Inn* (25 miles from Invermoriston). Hence the way is down through Glen Shiel to **Sheil Bridge**, at the head of Loch Duich. Dominated to the west by The Saddle (3,317 feet), to the east by Sgurr Fhuaran (Scour Ouran, 3,505 feet), the highest of the Five Sisters of Kintail, Glen Sheil was the scene of the overthrow of the small 1719 Jacobite Rebellion, in which Spanish troops participated.

To Glenelg (9 miles).—From Sheil Bridge (*Hotel: Youth Hostel*) a road runs along the western side of Loch Duich to the ferry (pedestrians and cyclists only) at Totaig, opposite Dornie and Ardelve. Another sets out for Glenelg by the arduous **Mam Ratagan Pass,** which by a series of sharp elbows with a general gradient of 1 in 7 carries one in 3 miles to 1,116 feet above sea-level—an awkward journey for heavy caravans in tow. The views are glorious. Half a mile short of **Glenelg** village, bear right for the ruined Bernera Barracks (built, like the road after the Rebellion of 1715), for the Youth Hostel and for the old-time ferry (*cars*) across Kyle Rhea to Skye (*see* p. 129). Beyond Glenelg the road is rough and hilly, leading in some 10 miles to Arnisdale, on Loch Hourn (bus from Glenelg, *see* p. 129); it soon crosses Glen Beg, a couple of miles up which are two notable brochs—Iron Age stone towers over 30 feet in height, in care of the Ministry of Works.

Loch Duich.—The Kyle road takes the eastern side of lovely Loch Duich, by Croe Bridge and a climb over to **Dornie** (*hotel*), where a bridge (1940) has superseded the Aird Ferry over Loch Long—a branch of Loch Alsh—to **Ardelve** (*Loch Duich Hotel*). Here, on a rock reached by a causeway, is the picturesque **Eilean Donan Castle,** a stronghold dating from the thirteenth century. Destroyed in 1719 after the battle of Glenshiel, it has been restored and is shown to the public (Monday to Saturday: *admission charge*). The road from Strome Ferry (*see* p. 125) comes in at Auchtertyre between Ardelve and **Balmacara** (*hotel, see* p. 113) from which a final circuit brings one to **Kyle of Lochalsh** (*see* p. 113).

Loch Duich is the western terminus of grand walks over the mountains. **Glen Lichd**, the foot of which is crossed by the road at Croe Bridge, near the head of Loch Duich, leads along the south-western flank of **Ben Attow** (or Beinn Fhada, 3,383 feet), and by following the Croe stream to the head of the valley and thence skirting the eastern shoulder of the mountain, one can drop into the head of Glen Affric, and by Lochs Affric and Beneveian reach Invercannich (p. 121). Slightly shorter is the path by Dorusduain and Glen Grivie along the north side of Ben Attow, which forms part of the wild Kintail Estate of the National Trust for Scotland. **Kintail House,** between Shiel Bridge and Croe Bridge, is now an hotel. Rough paths from Dorusduain, up the Croe, lead to the **Falls of Glomach,** the highest waterfall in Britain—370 feet in one plunge.

Resuming our journey on the west side of Loch Ness, we pass (3 miles beyond Invermoriston) the *Alltsaigh Youth Hostel,* picturesquely situated between the loch and the height of *Mealfuarvonie* (2,284 feet). Seven miles or so farther on is the curve of Urquhart Bay (the reputed headquarters of the Loch Ness Monster) and the road swings into **Glen Urquhart,** noted for its fertility and beauty. On a promontory at its mouth **Urquhart Castle** keeps guard. (*Open,* 10 *a.m. to* 7 *p.m.; Sundays,* 2-7; *admission charge.*) Originally built in the twelfth century, it was besieged by Edward I in 1303, and in its place his engineers erected the fortress whose crumbling walls we now look upon. The remains consist of a high surrounding wall, a square keep three storeys high, and four square hanging turrets. The loch directly opposite the Castle is 750 feet deep. A cairn commemorates John Cobb, who here lost his life (September 29, 1952) in trying to break the record in a jet-propelled speedboat.

The road rounds Urquhart Bay at the mouth of the Enrick, passing through Lewiston (*hotel*) and **Drumnadrochit** (*hotel*) amid charming scenery. (Bus service on weekdays between Glen Urquhart and Inverness.)

A good road runs up Glen Urquhart, passing Loch Meiklie, a mile long, to **Invercannich** (*hotel*), in Strath Glass (about 14 miles), whence one may go northward to Beauly; to the west lies the magnificent Glen Affric, which gives name to one of the most impressive hydro-electric undertakings in the Highlands, depending on the lochs Beneveian (lower Glen Affric) and Mullardoch (upper Glen Cannich). The scheme has spared Loch Affric itself, and has brought greatly improved roads to the approaches. A pretty (though hilly) road goes northward from Milton (in lower Glen Urquhart) through to Beauly (*see* p. 124); this road by-passes Inverness for motorists and others heading for the north and west.

Four miles from Temple Pier, on the northern shore of Urquhart Bay, is the village of **Abriachan,** charmingly situated above the loch, about 10 miles from Inverness.

At the north-eastern end of Loch Ness is **Aldourie Castle,** the

birthplace, in 1765, of Sir James Mackintosh, the philosopher, statesman, and historian. A peninsula marks the division of Loch Ness from **Loch Dochfour,** a delightful little loch with finely wooded banks.

On the western shore are **Dochfour House** (a modern Italian mansion) and an *Obelisk* in memory of Evan Baillie, founder of the fortunes of the family of Baillie of Dochfour. At **Dochgarroch Lock** the Canal begins again. On out left as we enter Inverness rises **Tomnahurich** (the "Hill of the Boat," or the "Fairies' Hill"), the site of a remarkable cemetery (*see* p. 123). The Canal by-passes Inverness and reaches the Beauly Firth at Muirtown near Clachnaharry.

Inverness

Airport.—At Dalcross, 8 miles east. B.E.A. booking-office in Queensgate, Inverness.
Distances.—Aberdeen, 104 miles; Edinburgh, 156; Fort William, 66; Glasgow, 169; Kyle of Lochalsh, 81; Perth, 116.
Early Closing.—Wednesday.
Golf.—*Inverness Golf Club*, 18-hole course, at Culcabock, about ¾ mile south of the town; 18-hole municipal course at Torvean, ¾ mile west.
Guide Book.—See the *Red Guide to Inverness and Northern Scotland* in this Series.
Hotels.—*Caledonian, Douglas, Station, Drummossie, Cummings, Albert, Palace, Royal,* etc.; unl. *Columbia, MacDougall's* and many others. *Youth Hostel* in Old Edinburgh Road.
Public Library, Museum and Art Gallery.—Castle Wynd.
Population.—About 34,500.

Inverness, the northernmost town of any considerable size in Scotland, occupies a beautiful site at the head of the Moray Firth and at the north-eastern end of the Great Glen, which contains the Caledonian Canal. The river *Ness* divides the town into two portions, the larger being on the eastern bank.

The best views are from the boulevard along the western bank of the river and from the esplanade of the County Buildings. The latter, built of red sandstone, are generally spoken of as The Castle, although the Castle that figures in *Macbeth* (as well as the earlier residence of King Brude, according to some) is believed to have stood on the summit of the ridge to the east of the station.

Beside the Town Hall, which is at the foot of Castle Hill, is the **Town Cross.** The lower part incorporates a curious blue lozenge-shaped stone, called the *Clach-na-Cudainn*, "the stone of the tubs," and for centuries regarded as the palladium of the burgh. It derives its name from having been the resting-place for the water-pitchers of bygone generations of women as they passed from the river. It is said to have been used by the earlier Lords of the Isles at their coronation.

The last house on the right of Bridge Street (as one goes towards the river) is **Queen Mary's House.** It is so called from the tradition that Queen Mary lived in it in September, 1562, when the Governor of the Castle refused her admission.

On the western bank of the river, nearly opposite Castle Hill, is **St. Andrew's Cathedral** (Episcopalian), the most imposing ecclesiastical structure in the place. Its style is Decorated Gothic, from designs by Alexander Ross, LL.D., himself an Invernessian. Behind it is the park in which was formerly held the **Northern Meeting.** This function (instituted in 1788) consisted of Highland Games and Balls held in September, the latter being the chief social event of the Highlands. Piping Championships and Ball are now held in September.

About three-quarters of a mile up the river are the wooded **Islands,** connected with each other and with the roadway on either bank by suspension bridges, and forming a favourite resort in the summer evenings.

Not less worth a visit is the Cemetery on fairy-haunted **Tomnahurich Hill,** a thickly wooded height rising 223 feet above the level of the sea, and commanding good views. Another good viewpoint is **Craig Phadrig** (550 feet), on the farther side of the Canal. On top is a vitrified fort, identified with the home of the Pictish King Brude, who is said to have been visited here in the sixth century by St. Columba and converted to Christianity.

For fuller details respecting the town and for Culloden and the region east and south of Inverness, *see* the *Red Guide to Northern Scotland* in this series.

The route from Inverness to Fort William by the Great Glen is described in the reverse direction on pp. 115-122.

INVERNESS TO KYLE OF LOCHALSH

Skirting Beauly Firth, rail and road come, 10 or 12 miles from Inverness, to **Beauly** (pronounced *bew'li*). Some 2 miles before Beauly is reached the by-pass road from Glen Urquhart (*see* p. 121) comes in from the south. Beaufort Castle, the home of Lord Lovat, chief of the Fraser clan, is seen on the left as Lovat Bridge is approached. Beauly, a mile beyond the bridge, has the ruins of a thirteenth-century Priory. At **Muir of Ord,** 2 miles farther on, the quickest road to the west (*via* Orrin and Moy bridges) cuts away from the main north road. Beyond Marybank the conical Tor Achilaty (in a State forest) is kept on the left, and Contin is passed on the way to Garve (28 miles from Inverness), with the picturesque *Falls of Rogie* on the right of a short steep hill. Rail passengers go on past Muir of Ord to Dingwall, then west by Achterneed Station (2 miles from Strathpeffer, which has hotels and a Youth Hostel, buses, but no passenger rail service) to **Garve** (*hotel*). Road and rail re-unite a few miles short of Garve and for most of the way to Kyle of Lochalsh keep close company. **Loch Garve** is 1¾ miles long by ¾-mile broad. From Garve, a bus runs north-west to Ullapool (*see* p. 128).

Loch Luichart, a few miles beyond Garve on the left, measures about 5 miles in length. Its outfall forms a series of cascades, called the **Falls of Conon.** Beyond the head of Loch Luichart we pass the entrance to Glen Grudie and cross the *Grudie*.

At the Falls of Conon is one of the early hydro-electric schemes (now greatly expanded), forming a link in a vast chain of dams, pipe-lines, tunnels, and power-stations which lay under contribution the water power of a wide district extending from Loch Fannich, past Grudie, Loch Luichart, and Tor Achilaty, to the River Orrin.

We enter Strath Bran, to the south of which are the three fine peaks of **Sgurr a'Mhuilinn** or **Scuir Vuillin** (the highest 2,845 feet), and to the north-west the steep slopes of **Fionn Bheinn** (3,059 feet). West of **Achnasheen** (*hotel*), our road branches to the left and after passing Loch Gowan and Loch Sgamhain, with **Moruisg** (3,026 feet) to the south, leads down Glen Carron to Achnashellach (*Youth Hostel*) and **Lochcarron** (*Lochcarron*; unl. *Loch Villa*) or *Jeantown*, the "Kirk town" of the district.

The railway parts company with the road ere reaching **Strath-carron** Station (*hotel*) and skirts the southern shore of Loch Carron, on its way to Kyle to Lochalsh, passing the attractive village of **Plockton** (*hotel*); but the road keeps to the north side, ending at Strome Castle (National Trust; *Youth Hostel*), opposite **Strome Ferry** (*hotel*) (ferry, weekdays; 8 a.m. to 9 p.m. or dusk, October to May 9 a.m. to 5 p.m. or dusk; uniform charge for cars). From the other end of the ferry roads lead to Ardelve and Dornie and to **Kyle of Lochalsh,** about 80 miles from Inverness and ½-mile from Skye (*see* p. 129).

Lochcarron to Shieldaig and Applecross.—From Lochcarron village a road strikes sharply up the hillside and for some miles runs through grandly rugged scenery to **Kishorn** (*Youth Hostel*) and **Tornapress,** at the head of Loch Kishorn (where the Applecross road—*see* below—diverges on the left). The Torridon road continues northward through the romantic **Glen Shieldaig**, with its overhanging cliffs from four to five hundred feet high. Near the centre of the pass is a fine waterfall. The final portion of the road (18 miles) is through lovely woods to **Shieldaig** (*hotel*) on Loch Shieldaig, a branch of **Loch Torridon,** which is surrounded by scenery of great grandeur and beauty, with the very ancient red Torridonian sandstone much in evidence. There are hill roads (not available for cars) to the village of **Torridon,** at the head of Upper Loch Torridon, whence a road runs to Kinlochewe. Loch Torridon, stretching for 20 miles into Western Ross, opens out some of the wildest scenery in the West Highlands. The mountains around its upper portion rise to over 3,000 feet, the finest of them being **Ben Alligin** (3,232 feet), **Liathach** (3,456 feet), and **Ben Eay** or **Eighe** (3,309 feet), this last declared a "Nature Reserve" in 1951. On the north shore of Loch Torridon are two Youth Hostels—Inveralligin and Craig, not easily accessible.

At Tornapress the road to Applecross by the *Bealach nam Bo* branches off to the left. This road, which reaches a height of 2,053 feet, is one of the steepest—and yet grandest—in Scotland. It is emphatically *not* a route for caravans or large or overladen cars, not merely on account of the gradient (the road rises from sea-level to over 2,000 feet in just over 5 miles), but because the final stages of the ascent include a series of hairpin bends of such sharpness that very few cars can

125

negotiate in "one go." Once over the summit one has a really magnificent view across the sea to Skye from this ardous "Pass of the Cattle."

Applecross (*unlicensed hotel*) is placed at the head of a small bay. The principal occupations are boating and fishing, but there are some splendid walks—particularly to Loch Shieldaig. *Lonbain Youth Hostel* is 8 miles north of Applecross by bridle path. Every morning (except Sundays) a vessel sails from Toscaig, 4 miles south of Applecross, to Kyle of Lochalsh and returns in the afternoon.

ACHNASHEEN TO GAIRLOCH

Leaving Achnasheen the road (A832) skirts the north side of Loch a'Chroisg (Rosque), rises to the summit (815 feet) and then drops rapidly into *Glen Docherty*, a wild and narrow ravine, bounded by steep and lofty mountains. We emerge at the scattered village of **Kinlochewe** (*hotel*), about 2 miles from the head of Loch Maree and 10 miles from Torridon (bus from Achnasheen). Close to the shore of Loch Maree, we travel to *Bridge of Grudie*, 4 miles from which is **Talladale** (*Loch Maree Hotel*), situated half-way along the western bank.

Loch Maree, one of the finest lochs in Scotland, is about 12 miles long and from 1 to 3 miles broad. The river Ewe flows from it and enters the sea at Poolewe (*see* p. 127). On both sides of Loch Maree are lofty mountains. Those on the northern shore rise almost perpendicularly, and are of a singularly bold and severe aspect. The most conspicuous is **Slioch** (3,260 feet), which presides over the loch. On the southern side **Ben Eay** or **Eighe** (3,309 feet), one of the Torridon group (*see* p. 125), towards the upper end of the loch, attracts special attention by its peaks of white quartz and its beautiful form. It is included in Britain's first National Nature Reserve (1951).

The surface of the loch is broken mid-way by some twenty or more islands. **Eilean Subhainn** is a mile in length. On it are three lochs. **Garbh Eilean** ("rough island") and **Eilean Ruaridh** (pron. "rory"), towards the west, are generally regarded as the most beautiful. The most celebrated island—Isle Maree—lies near the northern shore and contains a primitive burying ground and ruins of an ancient chapel, said to have been erected in the seventh century by St. Malruba, a monk of Bangor (in Ireland), the tutelary saint of the district, after whom the loch and island are named. On the island is an old wishing tree and a well said to have healing properties.

About 2 miles from the widest part of the loch we turn inland and come to the **Kerry Falls,** with yet another hydro-electric scheme in operation. Then the lovely Pass of Kerrysdale is traversed and we reach the west coast at Gairloch.

Gairloch

Access.—Gairloch is 73 miles from Inverness *via* Achnasheen (30 miles) on the Dingwall-Kyle of Lochalsh railway line, from which it is reached by bus. By the more northerly route, *via* Poolewe, Gruinard Bay, Dundonnell, Braemore, and Garve, it is 92 miles to Inverness. In the season this makes a favourite round trip from Inverness. Buses connect Gairloch with Poolewe and Aultbea on Loch Ewe and with Laide on Gruinard Bay.

Gairloch (*hotel*) is the centre of a beautiful district, with a genial climate. Its facilities for boating and bathing, fishing (in the Bay: trout and salmon in nearby lochs and rivers) and golf (9-hole course) make it a favourite resort and tax its accommodation resources. There is a Youth Hostel at Carn Dearg, 4 miles away, on the northern shore of the Gairloch.

In addition to Kerrysdale and Loch Maree, places of interest within easy reach include the charming village of **Flowerdale** and Flowerdale House, an eighteenth-century mansion, between the large hotel and the pier; the picturesque northern and southern coasts of the loch; and the unique Inverewe Garden (7 miles)—best seen in spring or early summer.

Gairloch to Ullapool.—The road (A832) continues northward through superb scenery, by Loch Tollie, **Poolewe** (*hotels*) and **Inverewe,** where is located the famous sub-tropical Garden (60 acres) presented to the National Trust by the daughter of its creator, Osgood Mackenzie, author of *A Hundred Years in the Highlands.* (Open 10 a.m. to dusk, Sunday 1 p.m. to dusk: admission charge: restaurant). Passing along the side of Loch Ewe—which played an important rôle in wartime—we reach **Aultbea** (*hotel* and *Youth Hostel*) and cross to Laide and down sharply by a notorious hairpin bend to **Loch Gruinard,** one of the grandest of West Highland sea lochs, with golden sands and solitary dunes—but no camping allowed. After skirting the loch

127

westwards, we climb over to **Little Loch Broom** at Badcaul and go up it to **Dundonnell** (*hotel: Achtascailt Youth Hostel*) at its head, with rugged red **An Teallach** (3,483 feet), "The Forge," towering to the south. A long ascent to over 1,000 feet takes us up Strath Beg and then we run down south-eastwards to join the Garve-Ullapool road (A835) at **Braemore** (45 miles from Gairloch), beside the Corrieshalloch Gorge and the magnificent **Falls of Measach** (150 feet: National Trust property).

From Braemore one can go northward down Strath More to lengthy **Loch Broom,** near the entrance to the inner portion of which stands Ullapool (12 miles from Braemore), or one can turn southward for Garve and Inverness.

Ullapool (pop. *c.* 650: *Royal, Caledonian, Morefield, Drumrunie Lodge*; numerous Guest Houses and *Youth Hostel*) was first established by the British Fisheries Association in 1788. Visitors may enjoy good bathing and boating, sea-fishing and trouting, and fine trips—by motor-boat or bus—to **Achiltibuie** (*hotel: Achininver Youth Hostel*), opposite the **Summer Isles,** the scene of Dr. Fraser Darling's *Island Farm* and *Island Year*. Achiltibuie is a good centre for climbing the Coigach peaks, of which Ben More Coigach (2,438 feet) is the highest.

For the entrancing region to the north of Loch Broom—a region teeming with lakes and dotted with striking isolated mountains, such as Suilven, the "Sugarloaf," readers are referred to our *Red Guide to Northern Scotland*.

Braemore to Garve (20 miles).—The road (A835) runs southeastwards through the desolate pass of Dirrie More, reaching the watershed between Atlantic and North Sea beyond Loch Droma (905 feet above sea-level) and descending to *Alguish Inn* (10 miles) in the heart of a wild and sombre region to the west of Ben Wyvis—somewhat altered of late by the construction of Glascarnoch Reservoir for hydro-electric purposes. For the last few miles the *Black Water* conducts us down to **Garve.** Garve (*hotel*) is 30 miles from Inverness by rail (*via* Dingwall) and 28 miles by road (*see* p. 124).

Skye

Access.—There is no service to Skye by *Air*. By *rail* and *boat* the shortest and cheapest route from Glasgow, Edinburgh, and the South is by Mallaig, terminus of the West Highland line extension (1901) from Fort William. All the year round MacBrayne's car ferry maintains services to and from Armadale in the south of Skye. In the season (June-September) motor-boats make several crossings (30 minutes) on weekdays between Mallaig and Armadale. Reservations are desirable on the car ferry and should be made as far in advance as possible to David MacBrayne Ltd., Mallaig. Tel: Mallaig 23. Rates for cars are considerably higher on this service than the Kyle of Lochalsh-Kyleakin ferry. Armadale is connected by bus with Broadford and Portree.

The alternative rail route *via* Inverness and the Dingwall-Skye line to Kyle of Lochalsh, if longer, offers attractions of its own and in some cases may prove more convenient. Circular return tickets are available in summer.

By Road.—The main approach to Skye, particularly for motorists, is from Kyle of Lochalsh, between which and Kyleakin there is a continuous daily Ferry Service. This operates—weather permitting—between 7 a.m. and 9.45 p.m. from May to September, from 8 a.m. to 8.45 p.m. in other months. The passage takes only about 10 minutes. The ferry boats have turntables. For cars the charge is according to horsepower (over or under 12 h.p.).

From Fort William, Kyle is reached by leaving the Inverness road (A82) at Invergarry (25 miles) and turning north-westward (by A87) for Cluanie, Glen Shiel, and Loch Duich. Coming from Inverness, one strikes westward at Invermoriston (28 miles) near the southern end of Loch Ness, and runs up Glen Moriston (A887) to join the Invergarry road at Loch Cluanie. The road from Inverness which follows the railway route to Kyle of Lochalsh *via* Garve and Achnasheen (A832) and southward by Loch Carron (A890) involves a ferry crossing at Strome.

The ferry from Glenelg to Kylerhea carries pedestrians and cyclists daily except Sunday. Small space available for cars operating from mid April to end of September, 8.30 a.m. to 8 p.m. or dusk if earlier.

Buses.—MacBrayne runs buses on weekdays between Kyleakin, Broadford, and Armadale and in summer between Armadale, Broadford, Sligachan, and Portree. Other operators also have services from Kyleakin to Dunvegan, to Portree, to Luib; from Portree to Kilmaluig (*via* Kilmuir and Uig: or *via* Staffin and Flodigarry), to Dunvegan, Borreraig and Glendale, to Sligachan and Glenbrittle, etc. The principal places are thus linked with one another and with the ferry ports, but as some buses go only on certain days and in certain seasons and subject to various conditions, the use of current local time-tables is essential.

Motor-coaches make whole day, afternoon, and evening excursions round or across Skye from Kyleakin, Broadford, and Portree during the season.

So much has been written regarding the misty mountains of Skye that it is desirable to stress the fact that the attractions of the island are by no means solely for climbers. Some of the roads have been rebuilt, and almost every one of them commands grand views, so that motorists can enjoy fine scenery without any physical effort, though careful driving is required. Moreover, the traffic-stream is not so heavy as to make either cycling or walking along these roads unpleasant, and in addition there are innumerable byways leading to outlying corners of the island which are well worth exploration. Mountain-climbing in the Coolins is perhaps the chief holiday attraction, but Skye has boating of all kinds, bathing, fishing, golf, tennis, and Portree has a mobile cinema, while the Games are an important fixture. In 1950 was instituted "Skye Week" (usually at the end of May), intended to be an annual period of "festivities and typical Hebridean celebrations"—Highland games, ceilidh, piping competitions, etc. The island is steeped in Celtic and Norse folklore and memories of clan rivalries (Macleods in the north versus Macdonalds in the south) and crofters' struggles, of Flora Macdonald and Prince Charles's perilous wanderings, and of the visit of Dr. Johnson, who composed Latin odes in praise of Skye.

Nor should the weather, however notorious, act as a deterrent. There are wet days, as in all mountainous districts (and visitors should not go unprepared for them), but there are also many fine days, particularly in June and September. Indeed, Skye sometimes enjoys sunny spells when the weather conditions are bad in other regions.

By far the largest of the Inner Hebrides (643 square miles: population 8,100), the island is of extremely irregular shape, some 50 miles from end to end with a width varying from 4 to

25 miles. As the map shows, it consists of a central nexus, on which Portree and the Coolins, and a number of long peninsular arms intersected by wild sea-lochs. Hence its name, the Winged Isle (Gaelic, *Eilean Sgiathanach*)—though others derive it from Norse *ski*, a cloud.

Skye has a long history, mingling with prehistory (of which there are relics) and legend. St. Columba visited the island in the sixth century, and for four centuries and more—till the battle of Largs in 1263—it was under the sway of the Norsemen, as many place-names testify. Clan warfare went on through succeeding centuries, to be followed by a no less dire struggle against economic difficulties, largely of an agrarian nature, culminating in a crofters' "Rising" in the 1880's. For over a century depopulation and emigration have left vacant many a "lone shieling of the misty island" and many of Skye's best sons have sought (and made) their fortunes afar.

Most of the people are still crofters, but earning a living by other means where possible. Fishing is hardly an industry now but cattle and sheep are sent to the markets on the mainland. Of growing importance is the tourist industry: the island has some excellent hotels, many good boarding-houses, and four Youth Hostels (much frequented in the season). Since the opening of the Storr Lochs Hydro-Electric Scheme in 1952 (*see* p. 140) electricity is becoming more generally available, while many of the usual amenities are greatly improved.

Visitors who cross from the mainland by the Kyle of Lochalsh ferry land at—

Kyleakin

a pleasant little village bordering the broad strip of green turf through which the road runs and with grand views across the Kyle, up Loch Alsh to the Five Sisters of Kintail. Kyleakin (pronounced *kyle-akin*) means Haco's Strait. Here the King of Norway passed in 1263, with his mighty fleet, on his way to defeat at Largs by the forces of Alexander III, aided by a providential October gale. Kyleakin has hotels (*King's Arms, Marine:* unl. *White Heather*) and is a good spot for excursions, fishing and boating.

Overlooking the pier is the ruined **Castle Moil** (or *Maol*), reputed to have been built by a Norwegian princess nicknamed "Saucy Mary," who stretched a chain across the Kyle and allowed no ship to pass without paying toll.

From Kyleakin to Broadford is a matter of 8 miles along a road commanding wonderful views, above all, of the incomparable Coolins. At Lusa the mountain road from **Kylerhea** (7 miles) comes in on the left. It is a steep, narrow road.

Four miles west of Lusa is—

Broadford

Bank.—Bank of Scotland.
Buses.—To Kyleakin, Portree, etc.
Distances.—Kyleakin, 8 miles; Armadale, 16½; Elgol, 15; Portree, 26.
Hotels.—*Broadford, Dunollie.*
Youth Hostel.—On north shore of Broadford Bay.

Broadford is the second largest community on Skye, though here and elsewhere on the island the houses and hotels are spread over a considerable area. The main portion overlooks Broadford Bay, where boating and fishing can be enjoyed. Broadford is a good centre for exploring the eastern portion of Skye, for from the village go roads to Armadale (A851) and to Elgol (A881) on Loch Scavaig.

Broadford to Loch Scavaig (15 miles).—This is one of the finest excursions on Skye. Immediately beyond the Broadford Hotel the Red Coolins spring into view, looking very shapely and forming a horseshoe. One could ascend the western end of the horseshoe and from it carry on over **Beinn Dearg** (2,323 feet) to **Beinn na Caillich** (2,403 feet) and down the latter, near which, at Corriecatachan, Johnson discoursed and Boswell caroused. But there is more remunerative outlet for energies close at hand. Go, for instance, a mile or so farther along the Elgol road, past the ruined church of Kilchrist and the neighbouring loch, and you will have a fine distant view of the Black Coolins. The road winds past the loch and through hilly pastoral country and then again springs a surprise in the shape of a full-length view of bewitching **Blaven** (3,042 feet), its eastern face riven with corries. The beauty of the view is intensified by **Loch Slapin,** in the fore-ground. From **Torrin** (or **Torran**) the road runs round the head of Loch Slapin—from which a path leads northwards through Strath Mor to Luib (3½ miles) on the coast road from Broadford to Portree—and then follows the eastern side of Loch Slapin past the entrance to Strathaird House and finally drops down to Elgol on the shore of Loch Scavaig. Westward, on the far side of the mouth of Loch Scavaig, lies the island of **Soay,** whose thirty or so inhabitants were transferred in 1953 to Craignure in Mull.

Walkers who intend to make for **Coruisk** should leave the Elgol road by a path which starts by the entrance gates of Strathaird House and goes nearly due westward, keeping well up on the hill-side to avoid the boggy ground below, and in 4 or 5 miles arrives at **Camasunary,** a farmhouse standing at the head of a little bay. Camasunary is an important meeting-point of routes: northward through Glen Sligachan to Sligachan Hotel; southward down the coast to Elgol (but this walk should be taken in the reverse direction, for the sake of the views) and westward to Loch Coruisk. This last walk is one of the excursions for which Skye is famed, though it may be well to warn strangers that the only ways out of the Loch Coruisk basin are over the mountains (*see* below) of by the path from Camasunary or by one of the boats bringing visitors from Elgol or Glenbrittle. From Camasunary take the narrow path on the far side of the stream, working round the steep and rocky headland at a considerable height above the sea. The distance is not more than 4 miles, but the walk is extremely rough and is not recommended to those who dislike narrow and exposed paths. The worst portion of all is at the notorious **Bad Step,** where the rocks over which one passes shelve steeply to the sea. However, by climbing above the rock face one can reach a heather track running about 70 feet above the creek forming the Bad Step.

The road from Broadford ends at **Elgol,** a small and very scattered upland village (boarding-house and cottage accom-modation) from which there is a steep descent to the beach and what is probably the finest sea and mountain view in Britain—that up Loch Scavaig to the heart of the Coolins. About a mile to the south is **Prince Charles's Cave,** in which Lady Mackinnon entertained the fugitive Young Chevalier to cold meat and wine ere he set out for the mainland. To the north-west, beyond the head of Loch Scavaig, hides—

Loch Coruisk

Coach excursions to Elgol from Broadford and Kyleakin allow time to visit Loch Coruisk, a pack luncheon being indicated. Boats take parties from Elgol and Mallaig. Time is usually allowed for an exploration of Loch Coruisk and its immediate surroundings. Weather permitting, a landing is made during MacBrayne's weekly steamer excursion in summer from Mallaig (with train connection from Fort William; steamer connection from Kyle of Lochalsh and Armadale).

The real grandeur of this incomparable scene—the quintessence of Skye—is only to be appreciated in the course of the approach to it across the waters of Loch Scavaig. Loch Coruisk itself is not visible, but the great rocky amphitheatre in which it lies is mirrored in the waves and the whole picture is so satisfying that even the most daring artist would not require to take liberties with any detail of the grouping or colour. The identity of the various peaks can best be obtained from the map.

From the landing-place a few minutes' walk brings us above the end of **Loch Coruisk** ("Co*roosk*") and the view from this point is such that most people decide to have their picnic here and to explore the loch-side afterwards.

Loch Coruisk to Sligachan (7 miles).—The path to Sligachan is by the east side of Loch Coruisk as far as the Big Burn (say about half a mile). Here turn to the right and (keeping the burn and Loch Choire Riabhaich on the left) an easy climb brings one to the summit of **Drumhain** (1,038 feet—a grand viewpoint). A walk of roughly a mile along the summit of Drumhain in a north-westerly direction opens up a fine view of **Harta Corrie:** one of the wildest corners in the Coolins, hemmed in by steep black rocks extending from Sgurr nan Gillean on the right to Bruach na Frithe and Bidean Druim nan Ramh on the left (*see* p. 137). At the entrance to the Corrie the "Bloody Stone" marks the scene of the massacre (1601) of the Macleods by the Macdonalds.

The direct descent from Drumhain to Harta Corrie is not easy and one should therefore retrace one's steps to the cairn at the pass. From the cairn a track leads northwards across an eastern shoulder of the hill and then descends into Glen Sligachan and joins the Camasunary path at a point about 1 mile north of Loch an Athain. From there the long and tedious walk down Glen Sligachan begins, and it will take 1½ to 2 hours' steady going to reach Sligachan.

For the Coolins, *see* p. 136.

Broadford to Armadale (16 miles).—This run (by A851)

through the district of **Sleat** (pronounced *Slate*), Skye's southern-most projection, affords many excellent views of the mainland, the mountains around Loch Hourn showing up particularly well. Some 9 or 10 miles from Broadford is **Isleornsay,** a village beside an island (when the tide is in) with a choice of hotels (*Isleornsay, Duisdale; Ord House* unl.). A couple of miles further on is Loch nan Dubhrachan, noted for its "Monster" or water-horse. A headland near Teangue bears the ruins of Knock Castle—the Castle Camus of mediæval times. Beyond Kilmore (the Macdonald burying-ground) and Sleat Church we come to Kilbeg, where at Ostaig Dr. Johnson stayed with the minister. The present-day Ostaig House is the residence of Lord Mac-donald, whose huge Gothic seat, **Armadale Castle** (1815: designed by Gillespie Graham), towers in wooded grounds a mile to the south. Armadale is connected by steamer and motor-boat with Mallaig (*see* p. 110), about 5 miles across the Sound of Sleat. Ardvasar, a little to the south, has an hotel (bus to Broadford and Kyleakin).

A favourite excursion from Broadford and Kyleakin combines this route with a diversion over to the west coast of Sleat peninsula, leaving the main road at Loch nan Dubhrachan and returning to it at Ostaig. With magnificent viewpoints for the Coolins and the surrounding seas, this loop road (12 miles) goes across to **Ord** (*Guest-house*) on Loch Eishort, by whose rock-garden shores the poet Alexander Smith, author of *A Summer in Skye* (1865), had his base. Here the road turns south-wards, past the remains of **Dunscaith Castle,** a historic stronghold, originally built in a night by Cuchullin, according to *Ossian,* and recrosses Sleat from Tarskavaig Bay by Loch Dhughaill.

Broadford to Portree (28 miles).—This (A850) is one of the most interesting roads in the island, the views changing con-tinually and being almost throughout of a high order. The islands off the coast are Scalpay and Raasay, separated by Kyle Mhor, the "great strait." **Scalpay** bears the ruins of an ancient chapel on a Culdee site. **Raasay** is marked by the curious truncated cone of Dun Can (1,456 feet). The weekday mail steamer from Mallaig and Kyle of Lochalsh to Portree calls at Raasay, and there is also a ferry from Sconser.

Inland, as the road rounds Loch Ainort and then runs up the

southern shore of Loch Sligachan, there are innumerable glimpses of the Coolins, and fine distant views up the coast to the Storr Rock. Walkers will find a short-cut between Strollamus (4 miles from Broadford) and Luib, on Loch Ainort. This rejoins the coast road at **Sconser** on the southern shore of Loch Sligachan (*Sconser Lodge Hotel.* 9-hole golf course).

About 18 miles from Broadford is the *Sligachan Hotel*, an establishment famous as headquarters for climbs in the Coolins. The road straight ahead (A863) continues to Western Skye, but for Portree we turn right. From Sligachan Bridge the views of the Coolins are magnificent. For Portree *see* p. 139.

The Coolins

The Coolins (or Cuillins, the spelling Cuchullins being due to a fanciful derivation) undoubtedly provide the most splendid mountain scene in Britain. It is not a question of height or extent (for the highest point is but 3,251 feet above the sea and the main group measures only about 8 miles by 6 in extent), but of proportions, as a result of which the peaks seem to soar to a much greater height than they do in fact and possess a sublimity which is not encountered elsewhere in Britain. Formed of black "gabbro," a coarsely crystalline igneous rock, the Coolins, with their reliable footholds and handholds, offer some of the best rock-climbing in Europe.

It cannot be too strongly emphasized that climbing in the Coolins is dangerous for those unaccustomed to such conditions. The steepness of the routes is such that in several cases there is no feasible alternative route, so that if one misses the right path one is almost bound to get into difficulties. The one path which is quite safe for novices is that up Bruach na Frithe: almost anyone with sufficient energy can manage this in safety, given clear weather; as for the rest, one should take an experienced companion, a water-flask and an "iron ration" of, say, chocolate or biscuits in case of delay. The compass, owing to the magnetic nature of the rock, especially on the ridges, is quite unreliable, so that a sudden envelopment in mist may make descent dangerous.

The best known and most popular of the Coolins is undoubtedly **Sgurr nan Gillean** (3,167 feet)—"the peak of the young men"—all in all, probably the most difficult "tourist" mountain in Scotland. The easiest way up it has some steps, especially near the top, that are distinctly trying to the uninitiated.

The ascent from Sligachan will take 3 to 4 hours, and the descent 2 to 3 hours. From the hotel follow the Dunvegan road for a third of a mile; then turn off on the left by the track leading to Cuillin Lodge. Cross the Red Burn by the stepping-stones (or by a footbridge nearer the hotel) and keep southward over the moor. Loch a' Choire Riabhaich is passed on the left, and the Coire nan allt Geala is gained by a rough, steep, stone shoot. Progress up this corrie is over a wilderness of boulders and screes to the ridge which extends south-eastwards from the summit. This ridge is struck at a point about 300 feet below the top. From this the route lies along and up the ridge, dipping over to the left-hand side in places where the direct ascent up the ridge is too steep. Hands as well as feet will here have to be constantly used, and a sharp lookout for the small cairns which indicate the right route: the nail marks on the rocks, too, are a useful guide. A little short of the summit a gap has to be crossed, which at first sight seems a bit sensational; but the rock is firm and good, and the handholds and footholds excellent. The top is a very narrow one, with precipitous cliffs all around.

The view is remarkably fine, the extraordinary boldness and grandeur of the rock scenery in the immediate foreground forming such a magnificent set-off to the moors below and the "wine-dark" sea in the distance. The descent is exactly by the way you came up. A possible alternative is along the western ridge and over its tooth and then down a vertical chimney into Coire Bhasteir; but this route is very difficult (it requires the use of a rope) and must not be attempted except by a party accompanied by a good guide.

Bruach na Frithe (3,143 feet)—"the ridge of the forest"—is not so well known as Sgurr nan Gillean, but the view from it is, if anything, finer and it is much more easily scaled. The ascent should be undertaken only in clear weather. Time, about 4 hours up and 3 hours down. Turn off the Dunvegan road as for Sgurr nan Gillean (*see* p. 136) but instead of crossing the Red Burn at Cullin Lodge keep to the track which follows its left bank to the **Bealach a'Mhaim** (pron. *Vaim*, 1,132 feet). From here turn south up over the long grassy slope for about 1,000 feet, and then over easy screes and rock to the summit. On nearing the summit keep below the ridge a little to the right, and so avoid all difficulties. The descent can be made by the east ridge towards Sgurr nan Gillean, and then down into Fionn Choire, where the walking is smooth and pleasant. It is worth while when on Bruach na Frithe to go round the head of Fionn Choire to the Bhasteir and Tooth.

To **Glen Brittle** (14 miles from Sligachan by road, 7 miles by path).—Either by the rough and hilly road from Drynoch, on the Dunvegan road, or *via* the Bealach a'Mhaim, a delightful and easy walk of 3 hours or so from Sligachan (*see* under Bruach na Frithe, above). The track joins the road near the head of Glen Brittle. The view of the Coolins from the top of the pass is unsurpassed.

Glen Brittle rivals Sligachan as the mountaineering centre in Skye. *Glenbrittle House,* once a shooting lodge, is now an hotel, while there is a boarding-house in connection with the Post Office and a Youth Hostel (half a mile north of Glenbrittle House) with 80 beds.

There is a bus service to Sligachan (daily except Sunday) and Portree.

Coire Lagan.—The route up the burn which comes down just beside Glenbrittle House, near the foot of the glen, leads in about 2 hours into **Coire Lagan,** a scene of supreme grandeur. It is a rock basin, hemmed in by the cliffs and screes of Sgurr Dearg, Sgurr Mhic Choinnich, and Sgurr Alasdair, and containing some of the finest examples of glaciated rock in the kingdom. The burn is crossed a short distance above the house, and then, after keeping the burn beside you on your left for a little way—say 100 yards—bear away to the right until you reach a fair-sized loch—Loch an Fhir Bhallaich = "the loch of the spotted folk" (*i.e.* trout). Skirt along the side of the loch, and not far on in the same direction Coire Lagan will come into view. Bear round to the left a little, and continue straight up, making for part of the corrie. Hereabouts a judicious selection of the route will be necessary, but by looking about carefully, small direction cairns will be noticed, and here and there a slight track, and the nail marks on the rocks, which will all help you to hit off the easiest route. After a brief scramble up some extraordinary glaciated rocks you find yourself at the side of a small loch, amid a scene of the wildest grandeur (**Loch Coire Lagan,** 1,845 feet). The descent should be made by precisely the same way as you came up. Visitors to Coire Lagan should make a point of seeing the Cioch, a curious pinnacle projecting from the face of Sron na Ciche, on the south side of the corrie and a favourite objective of skilled rock-climbers.

Sgurr Alasdair (3,251 feet)—"Alexander's Peak"—is the highest peak in the Coolins, and in every way worthy of its reputation. The best route of ascent is via the Sgumain Boulder Shoot from lower Coire Lagan and then over Sgumain and along the intervening ridge between the two peaks. A "bad step" on this ridge can be avoided lower down on the Coire Ghrundda side. The descent may be made by a scramble down the Stone Shoot. The Stone Shoot is not easy to find and a guide is essential for all but thoroughly experienced climbers. Time from Glen Brittle, 5 to 7 hours.

Coire na Creiche, midway between Glenbrittle and Sligachan, is one of the wildest corries in the Coolins. Coire na Creiche signifies in Gaelic "the corrie of the spoil," the spot having been in the old days a rendezvous for freebooters with their booty. An easy half-day's excursion, but well worth a whole day.

The complete traverse of the Cuillin Ridge between Glen Brittle and Sligachan ranks as the premier mountain endurance test in Britain. Full details of the climbing routes in the range will be found in the Scottish Mountaineering Club's *Guide to Skye.*

Portree

Access.—By road from Kyleakin, etc. Daily (except Sunday) steamer service to and from Kyle of Lochalsh (about 2 hours) and Mallaig.

Buses.—To Kyleakin, *via* Sligachan and Broadford; to Armadale; to Kilmaluag, *via* Staffin and Flodigarry or *via* Uig and Kilmuir; to Dunvegan, *via* Edinbane and Fairy Bridge; to Sligachan and Glen Brittle, etc.

Distances.—Sligachan, 9 miles; Dunvegan (*via* Edinbane) 22, (*via* Sligachan) 35; Broadford, 26; Kyleakin, 34 Staffin, 17; Uig, 15, (*via* Staffin) 32.

Golf Links.—On west side of town. Nine holes.

Hotels.—*Royal, Coolin Hills, Caledonian, Pier, Rosedale*; numerous private apartments.

Although its population numbers just over 1,500, Portree is the most considerable community on Skye, with several good hotels, a high school and a wollen and tweed mill. The name means "The King's Harbour" and commemorates a visit of James V. It is a compact little place on a hill-side partly enclosing its Harbour—a bay on the picturesque Portree Loch, its entrance guarded by lofty headlands. Canon MacCulloch, author of *The Misty Isle of Skye* (1905), was rector of St. Columba's Episcopal Church, which contains a Flora Macdonald Memorial Window. The Royal Hotel occupies the site of the thatched inn where Prince Charles said farewell to Flora.

The immediate neighbourhood is well wooded, a few minutes away are heather-covered hills and beyond them are the glorious Coolins and to the north the extraordinary Storr Rock. Portree is an excellent holiday centre, with plenty of facilities for excursions by coach, bus, steamer, and motor-boat. Golf, tennis, fishing are available. At the end of August (usually) the Games attract visitors and there are balls.

Prince Charlie's Cave (5 miles by boat; motor-boat trips run from the Harbour) is unremarkable in itself, and—notwithstanding Thomas Duncan's well-known picture—it is doubtful whether it ever sheltered the Prince. The boat trip along the coast to it, however, is very interesting. The *Cave*, blocked by a stone and bearing an inscription outside, lies to the north of the harbour.

Apart from the obvious walks around the Loch and the claims of the Coolins, the first excursion from Portree is usually that to the **Storr Rock,** which lies beside the Staffin road (A855) about 7 miles away. The climb to the top (2,360 feet) is not the leisurely stroll it looks to be from the main road. At least 2 hours should be allowed for the ascent, and almost as long for the descent.

From Portree follow the Staffin road for 5 miles past **Loch Fada** and to the northern end of **Loch Leathan**—the "Storr Lochs" of the hydro-electricity undertaking (*see* below; fishing by arrangement). The Storr itself is in full view with its square-cut top and its Needle Rock, the so-called **Old Man of Storr** (a basalt monolith 160 feet high), on the right, within easy reach from the road.

The upper cliff of which the Storr forms the crown is best climbed by leaving the road at the far end of Loch Leathan and making away to the left for a stony little ravine, whence the ridge of the cliff begins to rise steeply for the mountain-top. The final climb is short and steep. Once on top you have only to mount the long grass slope which bends round the tremendous black precipices forming the seaward front of the hills.

For good walkers there is an alternative route *via* Snizort, on the Portree-Uig road (bus route): this is a long uphill walk rather than a climb.

There is probably no finer mountain and sea view in the north of Scotland. The distance is to a great extent separated from the foreground by a wide belt of sea, studded with rocky islands and islets. There is no huddled-up array of intervening mountains. Further, the top of the Storr Rock is a soft, velvety greensward—a charming spot.

The Storr Lochs Hydro-Electric Scheme (opened 1952) has involved the raising of the levels of Lochs Fada and Leathan by the building of a dam at the northern outlet of the latter. An aquaduct leads the impounded waters to a generating station at the mouth of the Bearreraig River.

PORTREE TO UIG *via* STAFFIN

If possible choose a clear day for this excursion, as one of its features is the magnificent series of views across the sea, first beyond the islands of Raasay and Rona to the mainland and then to Lewis and Harris.

For the first few miles the view is dominated by the Storr Rock, with the Old Man of Storr standing away to the right of the main mass. A few miles from the Storr the road crosses the head of the **Lealt Falls,** where a burn falls into a black chasm with

fine effect, and then, rising high above the cliff, is seen **Dun Dheirg,** a natural formation which looks exactly like a fortification buttressed with pillars of stone. A little farther and **Loch Mealt** comes in sight: this loch spills its waters into the sea by a fine cataract, but the note-worthy feature hereabouts is the rock-formation composing the cliffs, its alternate horizontal and vertical bands having given it the name of the *Kilt Rock*.

Staffin (*Staffin House*) is a scattered parish of smallholdings set out on the slopes at the foot of the **Quiraing,** one of the strangest and most fascinating mountains in Scotland. So broken is it into ridges and pillars that it resembles a mountain group in miniature rather than a single mountain. The former Staffin road through the Quiraing is now impassable for vehicular traffic and is only suitable as a footpath.

The direct road to Uig strikes west from Staffin and ascends steeply, with many sharp bends, to a high *col* (about 850 feet) between Quiraing and Biodha Buidhe. From the col it is a clear and fairly easy walk along the top to Meall na Suiranach (1,779 feet), but this route misses the most surprising feature of Quiraing —*The Table*—an area of smooth green turf sunk, as it were, into the solid rock until it is surrounded on almost every side by huge cliffs. There is, however, a fair path from the col to the Table along the eastern side of the mountain which leads to the Quiraing. It passes between the main mountain and the Needle and thence on to the Table.

Beyond Staffin Bay the coast road squeezes between the Quiraing mass and the sea and then comes to **Flodigarry,** where is an hotel occupying the residence built by a descendant of Flora Macdonald (*see* p. 142), who herself spent the earlier half

141

of her married life in the adjacent cottage (the cottage is courteously shown to visitors).

From Flodigarry we continue to Kilmaluag by a moorland road from which the land slopes gently down to the sea and affords magnificent views of Harris and Lewis. The "Flodigarry landslip," geologists tell us, is due to lava here sliding over clay. The west coast of this—the **Trotternish**—part of Skye is reached at **Duntulm** (*Duntulm Lodge Hotel*), where the scanty remains of the haunted castle—of old a seat of the Macdonald Lords of the Isles—rise gauntly above the cliff edge. Rather more than 2 miles southward a lane on the left of the road leads to the burying-ground of **Kilmuir,** where a large cross marks the grave of Flora Macdonald: this memorial has suffered alike from gales and souvenir-hunting tourists.

Flora Macdonald (1722-1790) was the daughter of a small farmer at Milton in South Uist. Even as a child she showed unusual talents and was taken with the family of Sir Alexander Macdonald of the Isles to Edinburgh, so that she might finish her education.
While she was visiting her brother at Milton, Prince Charles Edward landed in Benbecula in the course of his flight after Culloden (1746), and after some persuasion Flora agreed to help in his escape. On the pretence of going to visit her mother (who had married, when Flora was only 6 years old, Hugh Macdonald of Armadale), she obtained a passport for herself and a party which included "Betty Burke, an Irish spinning maid." Betty, of course, was the Prince in disguise. After a very rough passage the party proposed to land at Vaternish, in Skye, but on seeing militia there they landed instead at Monkstadt, the home of Sir Alexander Macdonald who had befriended Flora. Militia were at Monkstadt also, but arrangements were made for the Prince to spend the night at Kingsburgh, further up Loch Snizort, and next day he left by boat from Portree to Raasay.
Unfortunately Flora's part in the escape became generally known and she was arrested and sent to the Tower of London, whence she was released under the Act of Indemnity. Returning to Skye, she married Allan Macdonald of Kingsburgh and the pair settled down at Flodigarry. Here they lived for over 20 years, subsequently moving to Kingsburgh, where she was visited by Dr. Johnson. In 1774 the family emigrated to North Carolina, but Flora returned in 1779, her husband having been taken prisoner in the War of Independence. On his release they lived at Peingown, in Trotternish, until Flora's death two years after that of Prince Charles Edward. A treasured sheet from his bed at Kingsburgh served as her shroud.

In front as we continue southward from Kilmuir **Loch Snizort** appears, with Vaternish peninsula on its far side. Parts of the scenery hereabouts bear a striking resemblance to that in Norway—incidentally several of the rivers flowing into Loch Snizort Beag have names ending in "dal."

The road turning back to the left at the top of Uig hill is that crossing the Quiraing col from Staffin (*see* p. 141). We, however, keep to the right and as the road descends have splendid views of **Uig** village and bay. Uig is in fact a good place for a quiet holiday, with fishing, boating (Uig pier boasts of being the longest in Scotland) and a variety of excursions. It has an hotel and a Youth Hostel.

Beyond Uig the fjord-like ramifications of Loch Snizort are seen. On the right, after crossing the Hinnisdal river, are Prince Charlie's Well and **Kingsburgh,** with its memories of Flora Macdonald (*see* p. 142: the old house is gone), and then the road runs steadily down through Romesdal to Snizort and Borve and so to Portree.

Portree to Dunvegan (22 miles).—The outward jouney on the Dunvegan round should be made by Borve, Skeabost (*hotel*) and Edinbane (A850); travelling in the other direction (outward *via* Sligachan) one misses the magnificent views of the Coolins which are the feature of the run between Bracadale and Sligachan. The route between Portree and Dunvegan is pleasantly diversified with crofts, views across Loch Snizort and, as Dunvegan is approached, of the flat-topped mountains known as the Macleod's Tables (*see* p. 144). **Edinbane** (14 miles: *hotel*) is a quiet little place at the head of Loch Greshornish. At the **Fairy Bridge** (19 miles), where, we are told, a fairy sits at sunset singing to the cows, a road goes off on the right for **Stein** and **Trumpan** (on the Vaternish peninsula) and affords lovely views of Loch Bay (an opening from Loch Dunvegan), which appears to be land-locked by the long natural breakwater ending in Ardmore Point and the islands of Isay (offered to Dr. Johnson by Macleod) and Mingay. To the south-west lies the peninsula of Duirinish, terminating in the north in Dunvegan Head, a few miles from which, on Loch Dunvegan, is **Boreraig**, where of old the MacCrimmons, pipers to the Macleods, had their famous school of piping—a cairn now marks the spot. The fertile **Glendale,** which runs down to Loch Pooltiel on the west coast of the peninsula, figured prominently in the crofter "Rising" in 1884.

Dunvegan (*Dunvegan*: unl. *Ose Farm, and other accommodation*) is on the shore of Loch Dunvegan, with boating, fishing, and golf, but is mainly visited on account of its Castle, for over

seven centuries the seat of the Macleod chiefs. It stands to the north of the village on a rock having the sea on three sides, and formerly could be reached only by a boat and a subterranean passage, but access is now obtained by bridge. The Castle and grounds are open to the public April till mid-October (*Monday to Saturday*, 2-5 *p.m.; admission charge*).

Dunvegan Castle is said to have been founded in the ninth century, its high tower being added by the eighth chief, Alasdair Crotach, the hunchback (*see* p. 152), and a third portion being built in the reign of James VI by "Rory More," the twelfth chief. It is among the houses that claim to be "the oldest inhabited in Scotland." James V (1540) and Queen Elizabeth (1956), Johnson, Boswell, and Sir Walter Scott are among those who have been entertained within its walls. One of the treasures of the castle is a "Fairy Flag," which on being waved will bring relief to the chief or any of the clan. The charm was to act three times and has twice been employed. Among other relics are the drinking horn of "Rory More," MacCrimmon pipes, and a lock of Prince Charlie's hair. Dame Flora Macleod of Macleod, the twenty-eighth chief of the clan, holds an Overseas Day during Skye Week.

Prominent across the loch are two isolated hills, called on account of their curious flat summits **Macleod's Tables.** Each is about 1,600 feet in height.

The first part of the run (25 miles by A863) from Dunvegan to Sligachan is of great interest on account of the views of **Loch Bracadale**—its coast extremely irregular and its surface sprinkled with islands large and small. Some of the cliffs are magnificent. At the southern extremity of Duirinish are **Macleod's Maidens,** three basaltic columns, the tallest 200 feet high. They rise sheer out of the sea, and are backed by cliffs from six to seven hundred feet high. Towards the southern end of the Harlosh peninsula is a Youth Hostel (Balmore House). Beyond Struan (*Ullinish Lodge Hotel*) and Bracadale village—whence an inferior road cuts over to Portree (11 miles)—we round the long and narrow **Loch Beag** and then have before us the first of the magnificent series of views of the Coolins which provide such a splendid culmination to the run. Down below on the right is Loch Harport. At its entrance, on the far side, is **Portnalong,** where weaving immigrants from Lewis and Harris set up their handlooms in 1923; nearer its head is Carbost, with the famous *Talisker Distillery*. At the head of Loch Harport is **Drynoch,** whence a road leads southward to Glen Brittle (*see* p. 137). From Sligachan to Portree is a matter of 9 or 10 miles.

The Outer Hebrides

Most northerly and largest of the Western Isles, Lewis with Harris lies some 25 to 40 miles from the nearest mainland. With a string of neighbours stretching southwards—North Uist, Benbecula, South Uist, Barra, etc.—"Long Island" makes up the **Outer Hebrides.** Lewis proper forms part of Ross-shire; Harris is in Inverness-shire, like the rest of the group, including remote St. Kilda. Regarded as the most important repository of the Gaelic language and culture, the Outer Hebrides appeal strongly not only to learned folklorists and philologists, historians, and archæologists, but also to artists and nature-lovers, anglers, sea-rovers, and all who enjoy getting off the beaten track.

The scenery consists chiefly of bleak stretches of bog or moorland, and is only saved from being monotonous by the numerous lakes and inlet of the sea, fine sandy beaches, and by picturesque ranges in Harris, South Uist and Barra.

LEWIS

Lewis may be reached daily (except Sunday) all the year round from Mallaig or Kyle of Lochalsh by MacBrayne steamer. By *Air*, Stornoway has a weekday service from Abbotsinch (about 2 hours) *via* Benbecula, and (on several days weekly) from Inverness (50 minutes).

The picturesque passage from Mallaig to Kyle of Lochalsh has already been described (*see* pp. 112-3). From Kyle the mail steamer takes between 4 and 5 hours to reach Stornoway, some 70 miles to the north, and if visibility is good one is never out of sight of land. When **Raasay, Rona,** and the north of Skye are left behind, we cross the **Minch,** with the **Shaint Isles** and the coast of Harris to the west, and make direct for Stornoway.

At the east side of the entrance to **Stornoway** harbour we pass the "Beasts of Holm" at Holm Point, where on New Year's Eve, 1919, over 200 Lewis men returning on leave were drowned, when the Admiralty yacht *Iolaire* was wrecked. In the centre of the harbour, reached by a causeway, is **Goat Island.**

Stornoway

It will be seen at once that Stornoway (*County, Royal, Caledonian, Crown*), the metropolis of this island outpost, is no mere Hebridean village but a town of some substance. The population (5,500) has doubled in the last hundred years. Its prosperity, however, is subject to fluctuations, in spite of the munificent attentions of several wealthy benefactors. The Stornoway herring-fisheries and kipper manufactures have long been famous; as, too, is the making of rough tweeds (*Harris tweed*), which are hand-woven on looms in numerous cottages throughout the island from yarn spun in the spinning-mills of Stornoway.

The two most outstanding sights are **Lews Castle** and the **War Memorial,** a square tower (80 feet high) on a commanding site.

The old Stornoway Castle occupied a site on which now stand Maritime Buildings, offices on No. 1 wharf. It had a stirring history while a fortress of the MacLeods, but was captured in the sixteenth century by the Earl of Huntly. It was a stronghold, too, in the time of James VI of Scotland, of the "Fife Adventurers," colonists sent from the Lowlands to the so-called "most barbarous Isle of Lewis." This project, however, was doomed to failure, the Fifers for once meeting their match! Much damaged by fighting, the Castle was restored, only to be finally destroyed by the soldiers of Cromwell who took possession of the town in the name of the English Commonwealth. (From this incident Stornoway's principal shopping street derived its rather surprising name—Cromwell Street.) The present Lews Castle was built during last century by Sir James Matheson, Bart. (1796-1878), of Achany and Lews, who purchased Lewis in 1844, and spent a large sum on its welfare, especially its roads, and on schemes to turn the abundant peat resources to account. In 1918 his descendant sold Lewis to Viscount Leverhulme (1851-1925), who likewise devoted a fortune to it, his main hope being to develop the fishing industries (including canning) on modern industrial lines. In 1923, being forced to desist, he turned his attenion towards Obbe in Harris, presenting Lews Castle and grounds to the people of Stornoway. The Castle has been converted into an important technical

147

school, with textile, engineering, and navigation departments. A golf course (18 holes) in the Castle Grounds adds to Stornoway's other attractions for the visitor—bowls, tennis, angling, boating, bathing, and a cinema.

A bronze plaque on the wall of Martin's Memorial Church (Francis Street) marks the site of the house in which Sir Alexander MacKenzie (*c.* 1755-1820) was born. A fur trader in Canada, he was the first white man to cross America from coast to coast, and after him the Mackenzie river (which he discovered) was named. In the Town Hall (Cromwell Street) a tablet commemorates Robertson Macaulay, founder of the Sun Life Assurance Co. of Canada, who was a descendant of the Macaulays of Uig. His son, Thomas Bassett Macaulay (1860-1942), who succeeded as the president of the Sun Life Co., was in his later years yet another benefactor of Stornoway. The *Macaulay Experimental Farm* on Arnish Moor was an attempt to reclaim peat land for agricultural purposes.

A stone bowl used for baptisms in **St. Peter's Church** (Francis Street) was brought from the Flannan Isles, and is one of the oldest fonts in Scotland. The bell is over three centuries old and the altar-piece is still older. The church contains David Livingstone's prayer-book.

At the top of Francis Street may be seen one of the buildings of the famous **Nicolson Institute,** a secondary school founded by the local family of that name.

Excursions from Stornoway

Lewis, an irregular shaped island, 60 miles long, has fairly extensive bus services connecting outlying districts with Stornoway. As time-tables, where they exist, are not always reliable, careful enquiries should be made. For the motorist and cyclist, some roads are fairly good, others are bad; all are narrow.

1. The most popular afternoon excursion is to **Arnish,** which may be reached by motor-boat across the harbour in about twenty minutes; or on foot *via* the Castle grounds past the Lady Lever memorial, skirting Arnish moor (4½ miles each way). The winding moor road begins at the bridge over the river Creed, proceeding until **Prince Charlie's Cairn** is sighted. It stands near

148

to the farmhouse where the Prince spent a night after Culloden. **Prince Charlie's Lake** is near-by, and here is a favourite spot to search for white heather.

2. On the way to **Tiumpan Head** (pronounced *Chumpan*), just beyond the narrow neck of land at Braighe, is the **Old Church of Eye**. Here nineteen chiefs

of the clan MacLeod lie buried. Inside the ruins is an effigy of an armed warrior, supposed to be Roderick, the seventh chief. There is also a marble slab to Margaret, mother of the last Abbot of Iona.

On either side of the neck of land are fine bathing beaches. (Bus services.)

At Tiumpan Head, the end of the Eye Peninsula, we come on the Lighthouse unexpectedly. This lighthouse proved of special interest to Prince Charles and Princess Anne during the Royal Tour in 1956. (*Open to visitors daily except Saturdays and Sundays*). From here the coast of Sutherland may be very clearly seen on fine days.

3. The only road northward along the rugged east coast is from Stornoway to **Tolsta**. Tolsta Head is 13 miles north-east of Stornoway. There are innumerable sandy coves all along the coast.

4. While a visit to the **Butt of Lewis** (25 miles by A857) can be made in a few hours, it is better to make a day-tour of it. The first part of the journey after Laxdale is across the island from east to west for 12 miles over the Barvas moor. **Barvas** village is scattered over a fair distance. Near Shader, the next village, is the chambered cairn and stone circle of **Steinacleit,** a notable ancient monument belonging to the Neolithic Age (*c.* 2000 B.C.). The main road ends at Port of Ness, a mile or two south-east of **Eoropie.** Ten minutes' walk from this village is the Butt of Lewis Lighthouse. It was built by the father of Robert Louis Steven-

son. The Eye of the Butt, a great hole in the cliffs, should not be missed.

On the road between the lighthouse and Eoropie, picturesquely situated in the middle of fields, stands the historic *Teampull Mor* or **Temple of St. Molua** (?14th century; restored 1910-1912; key at Eoropie store).

On an islet, north from Port of Ness, is the ruin of Dun Eistean, fortress of the Clan Morrison, former masters of these parts and the bitter foes of the Macaulays of Uig, western Lewis.

5. The "Carloway Loop" should be taken by those who are spending but one day on the island, since it provides the greatest variety of scenery in the shortest space of time.

The route to begin with is the same as that described in Excursion 4. Near Barvas we turn south (by A858), passing along the Atlantic coast as far as **Bragar**, noteworthy for a broch and a huge whalebone arched over a gateway. A little farther on at **Shawbost** there is an ancient mill worthy of a visit.

Carloway (12 miles from Barvas) has a splendid example of an Iron Age Broch Tower, the highest side of which must be 30 feet high. The circular wall is double with the space of a few feet between, in which the remains of a staircase are clearly visible. Dun Carloway is in Ministry of Works keeping, as are the standing stones of **Callanish** or **Callernish** (7 miles further south), which appear silhouetted high up on the skyline long before they are reached. The stone circle (37 feet in diameter) is complete, and is approached by an avenue (270 feet long) of megaliths. In the opinion of many eminent archæologists the stones are in some ways finer than those at Stonehenge.

The return (16 miles to Stornoway) is by Garynahine.

6. Lewis possesses many tales of folk-lore and legend, the quaintest ones concerning the districts of Ness and **Uig**. The latter is quite different from any other district on the island, being grand, rugged, wild, and sparsely populated. In an Uig village (Valtos) was born Coinneach Odhar, the Brahan Seer, a renowned Highland prophet of the seventeenth century. The route is by Garynahine across the Linshader district and up the shores of **Little Loch Roag**, scene of the Gisla hydro-electric scheme. To the north the island of **Great Bernera** (a lobster centre) comes into view. The island is connected with the mainland by a three-

arch bridge opened in 1953. This district features very largely in William Black's novel *A Princess of Thule*.

The village of Uig, on Uig Bay, is 34 miles from Stornoway. The parish includes the **Flannan Isles**—the Seven Hunters—over 20 miles out in the Atlantic. The unsolved mystery of the disappearance of the Flannan lighthouse-keepers in December 1900 is the subject of a well-known poem by Wilfred W. Gibson.

Many glimpses of the Minch and the mainland are to be had on the route south to Harris (A859); first down Loch Erisort and then down Loch Seaforth. The latter, which is remarkable for its strong tides and salt-water rapids, gave its name to a branch of the Mackenzie family who for over two centuries (1610-1844) owned the island; one of them raised the Seaforth Highlanders in 1793. At **Aline Lodge** (23 miles from Stornoway) is the boundary line between Lewis and—

HARRIS

Hereabouts the landscape changes; mountains and rocky mounds replace the machair land of Lewis. The road from Aline goes round the base of **Clisham** (2,622 feet high), the highest hill in Harris.

From **Ardhasaig Bridge** (33 miles) the main road crosses the narrow isthmus (under a mile) to Tarbert (36 miles) and continues southwards to Rodel (60 miles: bus from Stornoway).

At **Tarbert** (now connected by car ferry with Uig and Lochmaddy; *Harris Hotel*) the road takes a wide curve inland then back to the west coast at the magnificent white sands of **Luskentyre**. The western shore is followed closely to Rodel near the most southerly point. Scarista has a fine sandy beach.

Obbe (or **Leverburgh** as it is now called: *Rodel Hotel*) is passed on the way. Here for all eyes to see are the scattered fragments of a millionaire's dream. Obbe was intended by the first Viscount Leverhulme to be the centre of the herring fisheries of the Atlantic. Alas, the piers are literally rotten and the houses unoccupied. The harbour was a very dangerous one owing to the countless little islets in the Sound of Harris, and the treacherous currents.

The ruined cruciform St. Clement's Church is the chief attraction at **Rodel** (or Rodil). Viewed from a distance the architecture resembles strongly that of the Cathedral at Iona. The interior is perfectly preserved and there are many tombs of interest, one of which is described by the Royal Commission on Ancient Monuments as "the finest in Scotland." This commemorates Alasdair "Crotach" MacLeod (1547)," a thorn in the flesh of James V, who circumnavigated his kingdom to reduce the islesman's pride."

The other road from Ardhasaig Bridge leads westwards for a dozen miles along the shores of West Loch Tarbert, with sudden turns and breath-taking vistas.

Amhuinnsuidhe Castle (pronounced *Ah-vune-suey*) stands on a quiet little bay sheltered by a peninsula. Sir James Barrie was often a guest here of the owner, Sir Samuel Scott, and many think that this peninsula was the original of the "Island that Liked to be Visited."

From Amhuinnsuidhe the landscape becomes more and more rugged as we proceed to **Husinish Bay.** A great stretch of white sand, it looks as though no footprint had ever crossed it. The view on a clear day is superb. The north is Loch Resort; close to the shore the island of **Scarp** stands out prominently, while to the south **Taransay** island and the higher hills of North Uist are plainly visible. A bus runs to Husinish from Tarbert.

North Uist

Lochmaddy may be reached by MacBrayne's car ferry service from Uig, with connections to and from Tarbert. Coaches run to Benbecula (p. 153) and its airport via the road causeway.

Loch Maddy is the chief of the sea lochs of North Uist (oo'ist). Its entrance is guarded by the **Maddies** ("the dogs" or "the wolves"), two craggy islets, 100 feet high. The township of **Lochmaddy** (*Lochmaddy*, *Newton House*) has a good pier at the head of the bay and is the capital of all the southern Outer Hebrides. North Uist has a loch for every day of the year, with sea trout and brown trout. From Lochmaddy a road goes round the north and west coasts by Tighary and another cuts across to

Carinish (11 miles: *Temple View*) at the south end of the island and to the **North Ford,** which connects North Uist with Benbecula. When the tide is favourable this Ford (nearly 5 miles) may be crossed on foot or in a vehicle—by those with local knowledge. A causeway with two bridges, using Grimsay Island as a stepping stone, was completed in 1960.

Benbecula

A small flat island linking North and South Uist, Benbecula (*ben-bek'-yu-la*) has no seaport of any consequence but it has an airport (Balivanich) which connects it on weekdays with Glasgow (Abbotsinch) and with Storno-way in Lewis. There is a coach service across the island, southward to Lochboisdale in South Uist and northward to the airfield, North Ford and the road causeway linking the island with North Uist.

From Gramsdale (*inn*) at the Benbecula end of the North Ford (*see* above), a road (A865) runs south to Creagorry (6 miles: *hotel*), crosses the South Ford (wadable at low tide) by a long single-track bridge—opened in 1942—to South Uist and so makes its way southward to Lochboisdale (27 miles). A road round the west side has magnificent long-distance views, on specially clear days St. Kilda being visible. On this side are the ruins of Clanranald's Borve Castle and Ormicleit; on the east coast is Loch Uskavagh, where Prince Charles landed when pursued by a man-of-war.

South Uist

South Uist is served from the mainland all the year round, on certain weekdays, by MacBrayne steamers from Oban, via Caslebay. Steamers arrive at Lochboisdale on Mondays, Wednesdays and Fridays at 7 p.m. MacBrayne buses run from Lochboisdale to the north of the island and on to Benbecula, where there is an airport.

At the southern end of the east coast **Lochboisdale** shelters in island-studded Loch Boisdale. Its hotel is well-known to anglers, South Uist being noted for the size and number of its sea trout. This coast is mountainous and deeply indented (Loch Eynort, Loch Skiport, etc.). Midway, in Glencorodale, between Ben More and Hekla—the island's chief heights, *c.* 2,000 feet— Prince Charles sheltered awhile in May-June 1746. The west coast, in striking contrast, consists of machair land, riddled with

153

freshwater lochs. Up it runs the road (A865) to Benbecula (21 miles; *see* p. 153) and Morth Uist (*see* p. 152). From Daliburgh (3 miles from Lochboisdale) a secondary road continues to Pollachar (*inn*) on the south coast. Seaweed in this region is dried and milled to powder by a factory at North Boisdale. A few miles north of Daliburgh, at **Milton,** is the cottage in which Flora Macdonald was born (*see* p. 142). Several lochs are skirted or crossed on the way to South Ford and the bridge over to Benbecula. The last of these, Loch Bee, which with Loch Skiport cuts off the northern tip of South Uist, is beside the experimental site chosen for the discharge of guided missiles. A huge statue of "Our Lady of the Isles" (by Hew Lorimer, R.S.A.) looks down from an adjacent height. Loch Druidibeg, south of Loch Bee, is in a Nature Reserve, a breeding ground for the greylag goose.

Conditions in South Uist—a sequestered home of Celtic folk-lore and the traditional West Highland crofting way of life—have inevitably been affected by the selection of the island (in 1955) as the base of a rocket range.

Barra

Although one of the Outer Hebrides—the most southerly of any size—Barra (*Castlebay*) is served, summer and winter, by MacBrayne's Inner Islands steamer (on Monday, Wednesday, and Friday) from Oban, which goes on to Lochboisdale in South Uist and returns by the same route, *via* Tiree, Coll, and Mull. On weekdays Barra can also be reached by air from Glasgow (Abbotsinch airport). A ferry service (no set times) operates between South Uist at Ludaig and the islands of Eriskay, and Barra.

On the roadless little island of **Eriskay,** between South Uist and Barra, Bonnie Prince Charlie first set foot on Scottish soil (July 23, 1745). The "Eriskay Love Lilt" is perhaps the best known of the songs of the Hebrides collected by Mrs. Kennedy Fraser. During the war (in February 1941) Eriskay was the scene of the wreck of the 12,000 ton *Politician*, with a cargo of nearly a quarter of a million bottles of whisky destined for America. Sir Compton Mackenzie humorously romanticised the consequences in *Whisky Galore*. The novelist lived in Barra for some years.

The small township of **Castlebay** (*Castlebay, Craigard*: unl. *Dunard*) stands at the head of a southern inlet, with Heaval (1,260 feet) in the background and, on a tiny island offshore, picturesque **Kisimul Castle**—a stronghold of the McNeils in ancient times, now part restored for habitation. Castlebay was once a busy herring fishing centre. Lobsters are caught and are flown to market.

Barra (8 miles by 5: population *c.* 1,800) is circled by a road (A888). West of Castlebay St. Clair's Castle occupies an islet in Loch St. Clair. Near Borve Point, on the west coast, are the ruins of St. Brendan's Chapel. From Cuier Manse and the original parish church of Barra—predominantly a Roman Catholic island—the road makes eastward for North Bay, where the airport is located. Minor roads run up to the Eoligarry peninsula, which shelters from the west the great *Cockle Strand*. Barra is noted for its cockle beaches, so firm that planes can land on them. Cockle-shell grit is exported.

On **Vatersay,** south of Barra, an emigrant ship was wrecked with the loss of 400 lives in 1853, at a period when perforce thousands were leaving their native isles. **Berneray** is the southern-most of the Barra Group. Its lighthouse, high on Barra Head, sends an answering ray to no less exposed and still more lonely **Skerryvore** (36 miles to the south-east), erected in 1844 by Robert Louis Stevenson's uncle, Alan Stevenson.

St. Kilda

Some 40 or 50 miles west of North Uist and Harris, St. Kilda was evacuated in 1930, but was reoccupied on being acquired (1957) by the National Trust for Scotland and leased to the Nature Conservancy. The chief island of the group is Hirta. Soay boasts a breed of sheep of its own, Boreray has the world's biggest gannetry. With its great cliffs, St. Kilda is a unique locus for bird-life study. As an R.A.F. rocket-tracking station, it will also be concerned with flying objects of quite another kind.

Index

Where more than one reference is given, the first is the principal.

INDEX